CHANGING BARNSLEY

From Mining Town to University Town

**Edited by Cathy Doggett
and Tim Thornton**

Wharncliffe Books

First published in Great Britain in 2009 by
Wharncliffe Books
an imprint of
Pen & Sword Books Ltd
47 Church Street
Barnsley
South Yorkshire
S70 2AS

Copyright © Cathy Doggett and Tim Thornton 2009

ISBN 978 1 84563 122 2

Typeset in the UK by
Mac Style, Beverley, East Yorkshire

Printed and bound in the UK by
CPI

Pen & Sword Books Ltd incorporates the Imprints of Pen & Sword
Aviation, Pen & Sword Maritime, Pen & Sword Military,
Wharncliffe Local History, Pen and Sword Select, Pen and Sword
Military Classics and Leo Cooper.

For a complete list of Pen & Sword titles please contact
PEN & SWORD BOOKS LIMITED
47 Church Street, Barnsley, South Yorkshire, S70 2AS, England
E-mail: enquiries@pen-and-sword.co.uk
Website: www.pen-and-sword.co.uk

Contents

Acknowledgements

The editors wish to thank all who have contributed to this book. Special thanks go to the former and current students and staff who are indeed 'the voices in the stone' and also to the artists in residence for working with us on the exhibition, Jessica Penrose (creative writer) and Chris Sedgewick (photographer).

Martyn A Walker would like to thank the Archivists at Barnsley Library and Mrs Hilary Haigh at the University of Huddersfield and Mr Martin Pritchard at the Association of Colleges in respect of the publication of the Barnsley Mining and Technical College floor plans. Particular thanks must go to Mr Ken Keen for permission to publish his photographs (plates 4, 5, and 6) and for his time in meeting with me in relation to the building and floor layout of the Mining and Technical College as he remembers them during the 1960s; also to Mr Alan Johnson of the University of Huddersfield for providing me with copies of the building plans. I would also like to thank Professor Tim Thornton, Pro Vice-chancellor, University of Huddersfield for his advice and support and Dr Roy Fisher of the School of Education and Professional Development for his comments, suggestions and ideas relating to further research into mining education.

Foreword

On 1 April 2002 the *Guardian* newspaper published an article describing architect Will Alsop's vision for Barnsley becoming a Tuscan Hill Town.

Immediately the newspaper's telephone switchboard was jammed with readers claiming to have spotted the annual April fool.

Not so! The joke was on them. Barnsley really was changing and Alsop's vision was fact, not fiction.

Had they gone mad in the Portland stone halls of Barnsley's Town Hall residents were heard to mutter.

Was Barnsley turning from mining beneath its green hills to stone town walls above them in one fell swoop?

Well not quite, but Alsop's ideas made us in Barnsley think about who we are and what we are to be in the future and we began our journey to become a twenty-first century market town. Nay, THE twenty-first century market town. No less ambitious than the ideas of Alsop himself.

In the late nineteen nineties Barnsley's reason for being was destroyed and we lost our identity. This new journey aims to recreate the sense of identity and purpose we once held so proudly as a mining community, but this time as a new place in a new world with new ambitions.

So what do we mean by twenty-first century market town – where do our ambitions lie?

Well, it's more than just a town with a market, albeit a very special one.

The concept of market towns is one of a place of exchange. An exchange of goods and services often grown or made locally. Hence our aim to produce, as well as retail, just as we did when our charter was granted in 1249.

But in a twenty-first century economy the exchange of ideas, knowledge and information is equally if not more important. So skills, education and learning will be a vital component of our new future.

This book tells of learning in our past and how it shaped people's lives in Barnsley. In particular it tells of the impact of the Mining and Technical College and our University Campus.

Ironically what was at the heart of our past learning will be the heart of learning in the future. The University Campus will be key to developing the skills for our new economy and helping us to raise our aspirations and ambitions even further.

It will provide opportunity to Barnsley people to achieve their dreams and for others from elsewhere to share their dreams with us.

Barnsley is changing – from mining town to market town. From a place built on coal to a place built upon enterprise and learning.

So when people ask me whatever happened to Will Alsop's Tuscan Hill Town, I tell them we're building it right here in Barnsley.

Cllr Stephen Houghton
Leader Barnsley Metropolitan Borough Council

CHAPTER ONE

Introduction

Cathy Doggett

'The past we inherit, the future we build'
NUM Banner Motto

It is an honour to write the introduction to this book which is the result of celebrations that were held in October 2007 to mark the seventy-fifth anniversary of the opening of an iconic building which had its origins in the coal mining industry as the largest Mining College in Britain, evolving in subsequent years to become, finally, home to the University Centre Barnsley (now renamed University Campus Barnsley) in the heart of the town. The University is very proud to be housed in such a magnificent building which, if the walls could speak, would have many tales to tell from across the years and indeed some from the present. As such, the celebrations of its history and current status were about more than bricks and mortar, they were about the people who have worked, taught and studied there during those seventy-five years.

The University Centre Barnsley is part of the University of Huddersfield. The main aim of the Centre is to combine educational development through widening participation with objectives for urban and social regeneration. Our goal is to offer Higher Education to students within their own community and in the spirit of partnership work to increase aspirations, develop courses and contribute to the local economy. Nevertheless, even though an enormous financial investment has been made in creating what is now a state-of-the-art university centre, the warmth and character of the building remains unchanged. Anyone entering the premises cannot fail to experience a sense of belonging and welcoming, perhaps a legacy that perpetuated the idea of the 'Voices in the Stone', a permanent exhibition which is housed within the Centre and was funded jointly by the Arts Council and the University of Huddersfield. In fact one can almost hear the echoes of past generations of students and staff.

Throughout the four weeks of celebrations the Centre opened its doors to the public, and during that time we were visited by many members of the community. These celebrations comprised the exhibition 'Voices in the Stone' as the central focus. To enhance the exhibition and mark the central subject area taught within the building over many years, mining, the public were invited to take a stroll down memory lane through a second exhibition of coal mining and coal mining education memorabilia, kindly loaned to the Centre by the National Coal Mining Museum for England and the University of Huddersfield Archives. In addition, events were staged that brought history to life for both adults and children, through living history performances staged by the National Coal Mining Museum.

In relation to the present, one of the objectives of the University Centre is to raise the aspirations of the children and young people of Barnsley, in particular towards progression to University. The celebrations presented an opportunity to foster an interest in the Arts. To this end a competition was offered across all the schools, the College and Community Learning Groups in the Barnsley Borough. Education establishments were invited to enter the work of children and young people. The competition was called 'My Barnsley' and pupils were asked to produce a piece of art work (in a medium of their choice) and/or creative writing that reflected Barnsley from their perspective. Our thanks are due to locally-connected individuals for judging that competition, namely, artists Ashley Jackson and Graham Ibbeson along with local historian and writer Mel Dyke, archaeologist and Egyptologist Joanne Fletcher and Robert Cockcroft, editor of *The Barnsley Chronicle*. This will now become an annual event.

Finally, the seventy-fifth anniversary was an opportunity to launch a series of public lectures that were the first in what will be another annual event here at the University Centre. This provides the public of Barnsley with the opportunity to hear eminent speakers who are experts in their subject area. Interestingly, as the reader will see in chapter three, these are actually not the first public lectures to be held here in Barnsley, the concept having been introduced here as far back as 1837. The content of this book includes a selection of chapters based on those lectures that were directly concerned with the history of this building or related topics.

In chapter two, Professor Tim Thornton, writer and historian, sets the scene around the history of the building, but more than that he provides a fascinating insight into the events leading to its opening in 1932. He captures a unique culture, steeped in history while demonstrating the forging of strong links between those involved with the mining industry in Barnsley and a commitment to the education and training of those working in that industry, a commitment that was to be sustained until the closure of the coal mines in the area. There is no doubt that the sense of partnership at that time is reflected throughout periods of the building's history, and that spirit of partnership is indeed very evident today.

In chapter three, educationist Martyn Walker takes us through the history and development of adult education in Barnsley within the national context. He discusses the somewhat turbulent history of the Mechanics Institute, its closing and opening on several occasions, moving from one set of premises to another amidst competition from other education providers of the times, until finally in the mid-nineteenth century seeing the foundations finally laid and charting this success through the establishment of the Mining and Technical College, through the days as a wider technical college as part of the Barnsley College to the present day as a Centre for Higher Education, now part of the University of Huddersfield.

Moving on to the building itself, that is University Centre Barnsley, and those whose lives have been touched by the activities therein, through three parts of a century, senior lecturer Lynn Rollin takes us through another journey, but this time through the eyes of an artist. She describes the build-up to what is now a permanent exhibition of photography and creative writing within the Centre, 'Voices in the Stone'. This celebrates those who have worked, studied or contributed to its development in some way. Her starting point is the unique importance and significance of our memories and story telling. She links this to how 'the seeds' of the exhibition were sown quite simply from the foundation stone at the side of the building, seeds which grew into full-blown celebrations of the building and its people. Lynn links the project to the art world, taking us through the process of photography and creative writing that is based upon some of the characters mentioned earlier who, generation by generation, have connections with the building and who have all contributed to the warmth and character therein which one cannot fail to sense on entering it. The chapter comprises a selection of the photographs taken from the exhibition and linked through pieces of creative writing based upon what former and current staff and students have to say. This truly gives the reader a flavour of what 'the voices in the stone' might well say about the past seventy five years if they could speak out loud.

Pete Birkby, senior lecturer in music and a professional musician, wrote chapter five following initial thoughts and the inspiration provided by his work on the composition of 'Voices', written and recorded at the University Centre here in Barnsley and played on the evening of the seventy-fifth anniversary as part of the celebrations. In order to write this piece, the composer researched seventy-five years of music 1932 to 2007. As the reader will see, in this chapter the writer tells us about the process, his thoughts during that time and how the music was developed. A copy of the CD is available on request from University Campus Barnsley. In addition to the music of the era, reflections on the final composition, the creation of the audio experience for the opening night and exhibition give the reader a glimpse into the world of the composer.

In chapter six, now moving out of the building but within in the same era, Jayne Dowle, writer, columnist and journalist, discusses aspects of the town of Barnsley. Taking us through the nineteen thirties and providing a 'feel' for the changes taking place in the town at that time concerning, in her own words, the town development, the evolution of civic pride and the identity of Barnsley in the nineteen thirties. As will be seen this fits well with the next chapter each providing different perspectives on the rich and dynamic social context within which the Mining College developed.

In the final chapter Keith Laybourn, born in Barnsley, the son of a coal miner and now Professor of History at the University of Huddersfield and one of the leading historians of twentieth-century Britain working today, provides a link between himself and Barnsley, giving a brief overview of the town from his perspective during his early years before moving on to explain how gambling was part of his early life and the culture in which he was raised: a chapter driven by personal and professional interest, and the strong sense of place which this book celebrates.

Giving us a brief taste of his childhood experience in one of Barnsley's communities, the writer moves on to a wider context, tracing the history of gambling during a significant part of the twentieth century. He demonstrates the role of a number of key parties, political and other, and how they influenced changes in the laws governing what appears to have been a popular pastime and feature of the times for a significant part of society. He clearly demonstrates how changes in law tended to affect working class people in the main ending with the changes that post Second World War liberalisation brought; this is a truly fascinating read about past times and culture.

CHAPTER TWO

Voices in the Stone: The Building, its People and Their Contemporary Resonances

Tim Thornton, University of Huddersfield

One of the advantages of anniversaries is that they invite one to take stock not just of the event commemorated but of its context and its resonances in the present. All the better when such an anniversary coincides with important contemporary changes. There is a danger, of course, of assuming continuities and connections when none may exist stronger that the inherent irrationality of an anniversary itself – where significance is attributed more thanks to decimal number systems than to a recognition of any real patterning of time. Contrast may be more important than similarity; conflict and tension more important than a smooth transition from past into future.

The detailed histories of the Mechanics' Institute and its successors the Technical College and the Mining College are described by Martyn Walker elsewhere in this book.[1] He explains how the Mechanics' Institute was re-founded on a secure footing in 1848, providing a service, as it did, in a large town of 15,000 people, yet one which was still then relatively isolated. He describes the introduction of Cambridge University extension lectures in Barnsley in 1884. The Mechanics' Institute opened its new building in Eldon St in 1878, with a lecture hall, reading room, library, museum and classrooms. He explains how it lost its prime responsibility for education, and in 1912 moved to Hanson Street, where it provided a library and newsrooms. Education courses by that

---

1. See below, pp. 22–53.

stage were the responsibility of the Technical School. Amongst other things, the Coal Mines Act of 1911 introduced requirements regarding education and training after the age of compulsory schooling, and established a Central Board for Mining Examinations.

Walker also explains how the Technical School already had six departments by 1910–11, with forty staff. He describes the existence of a separate School of Arts and Crafts from 1848; which became part of the new Technical School in 1908 (only to separate in 1935, retaining this independence into the nineteen sixties).

As Gosden and Sharp described many years ago, several centres of mining education were originally supported by the West Riding County Council, but then a decision was taken by the council to focus their support on the one location in Barnsley.[2] This meant a focus not only for all of what we know as the South Yorkshire coalfield, but also all of the former coal mining areas now in West Yorkshire. The effect of this decision was inevitably to lever much more money from the West Riding County Council into what became the Mining College.

Further, the West Riding County Council operated in collaboration with The Yorkshire College in Leeds (now, of course, the University of Leeds) and Firth College, Sheffield (now the University of Sheffield), both of which had very significant mining departments. The West Riding decision to focus on the Barnsley Mining School, therefore, meant the benefit of links with the Sheffield and Leeds departments, and the Mining School seems to have been developing successfully in the years before the First World War.

The newly created county borough council in Barnsley, however, tended to emphasise a more general development of the facility, which moved the focus away from strictly mining and into the provision of a more general technical college.[3]

---

2. P. H. J. H. Gosden and P. R. Sharp, *The Development of an Education Service: the West Riding, 1889-1974* (Oxford: Martin Robertson, 1978), p. 98.
3. Gosden and Sharp, *Development of an Education Service*, pp. 98.

Although the West Riding County Council then put investment into about half a dozen other centres of mining education, in places like Dinnington, Mexborough, Whitwood, the Barnsley College had by that stage achieved a significant scale and level of excellence.

1924 saw agreement by the West Riding County Council Education Committee to build a new Mining and Technical College; some years passed before this vision came to fruition, but in April 1930 the foundation stone was laid. It was opened on 10 October 1932 by Alderman H M Walker JP, the architects being Briggs and Thornely of Liverpool, the building contractor Charles Smith of Barnsley. The funding came from the Education Committee of the County Borough of Barnsley, which had been created in 1913. It was the proud boast of the time that Barnsley now had the largest Mining College in the country.

That then is the story: but what does it mean? Are there 'voices in the stone', and what story do they tell us?

There are important themes to draw out in terms of, on the one hand, the distinctiveness of Barnsley's culture and its local pride, with on the other hand its connections out into other parts of the coalfield and into both South and West Yorkshire, represented by the support of the West Riding County Council and the flows of students from across the coalfields through the College.

There are also important lessons in terms of a commitment to education. For this we might go back to the monastic tradition represented by Monk Bretton Priory, or to the free grammar school in Barnsley which dates from 1665; or to the founding of a philosophical society in the town in 1828.[4]

---

4. Claire M. Cross, 'A Yorkshire religious house and its hinterland: Monk Bretton Priory in the sixteenth century', in Simon Ditchfield (ed.), *Christianity and Community in the West: Essays for John Bossy* (Aldershot: Ashgate, 2001), pp. 72–86; Rowland Jackson, *The History of the Town and Township of Barnsley, in Yorkshire, from an Early Period* (London: Bell and Daldy, 1858), pp. 227–28, 232, 238–39.

We should also consider the structures and processes through which education could be supported. The Public Libraries Act of 1850 allowed councils to raise a rate to support a public library, and this and its successors Barnsley adopted in 1890. The town was incorporated only in 1869, so it was, in a municipal sense, way behind other longer established corporations, such as Manchester or, another pioneer in the north of England, Sunderland. There was, however, the Co-operative Library, one sign of the considerable influence of the Barnsley British Co-operative Society in a whole range of spheres.[5]

More important, however, are the social, economic and political networks which are so solidly represented by the building's foundation stones. These were laid in July 1930, and it is worth a particular consideration of one of the individuals involved and his context – that individual being Herbert Smith. Smith was born in the workhouse in 1862, and soon an orphan, adopted, as it happened by a couple of the same surname.[6] He started in the mine at Glass Houghton at age ten. In 1879 he became a member of the Glass Houghton miners' union branch committee, in 1894 checkweighman, and delegate to the Yorkshire Miners' Association. Service to the union led him to being, from 1896 to 1904, president of the Castleford Trades Council. In 1902 he was appointed to the joint board of the South and West Yorkshire Coalowners and Workmen, and 1906 was elected president of the Yorkshire Miners' Association.

Smith was active on a national and international stage. He served as president of the Miners' Federation of Great Britain (MFGB) (1922–29), campaigning for a minimum wage, an eight-hour day, the nationalization of the mines, and the

---

5. Alistair Black and Peter Hoare (eds), *The Cambridge History of Libraries in Britain and Ireland*, iii: *1850–2000* (Cambridge: Cambridge University Press, 2006), p. 178.

6. For Smith, see J. Lawson, *The Man in the Cap: The Life of Herbert Smith* (London: Methuen, 1941); Marc Brodie, 'Smith, Herbert (1862–1938)', *Oxford Dictionary of National Biography* (Oxford: Oxford University Press, 2004), *sub nomine*.

abolition of mining royalties. In 1914 he had been involved in the formation of the 'triple alliance' of workers from coal, rail and transport sectors. With Arthur Cook, MFGB secretary, he was prominent in the national miners' dispute which triggered the general strike of 1926.

He had a formidable reputation in mine rescue, even in his later years, for example in 1931, when nearly seventy, at the Bentley explosion, and in 1936, hearing of the Wharncliffe Woodmoor disaster while at a conference in Prague, travelling non-stop so that by 9 the following morning he was down the pit. Smith was also active in local electoral politics, and in 1903 won a seat on the West Riding County Council, focusing his activities on public health and education. In 1916 he moved to Barnsley, becoming a town councillor, and serving as mayor in 1932 – appropriately the year of the opening of the Mining College building. Smith's popularity, and the general commitment to the causes for which he stood, was demonstrated when he died, in his office at 1 Huddersfield Road, on 16 June 1938 – as his coffin was carried the 20 miles from Barnsley to Castleford cemetery on 20 June, crowds lined the entire route.

It is also important that the architect chosen for the project was one with a very major reputation and considerable skill. Arnold Thornely was a Liverpool architect who was involved in the creation of some of the major buildings in that city, including what is now known as the Port of Liverpool building (1904–07), originally the offices of the Mersey Docks and Harbour Board, and the India Buildings, completed for the shipping firm Alfred Holt and Co. in 1930.[7] Born in 1870, after qualifying he had commenced an independent practice in 1898. By the late 1920s he was achieving a much wider impact, including a commission for the new parliament building for Northern Ireland at Stormont (1927–32). He was knighted in 1933, a clear sign of the standing of the man who had been commissioned to design

---

7. Richard Pollard and Nikolaus Pevsner, *Lancashire: Liverpool and the South West* (New Haven and London: Yale University Press, 2006), pp. 71, 253, 341–42.

both Barnsley's spectacular town hall and new college.[8] Meanwhile, Charles Smith was the contractor responsible for many of the newly appearing council houses around Barnsley. In that sense, too, the project expressed another important manifestation of civic pride as the corporation took advantage of the sequence of housing acts passed from 1923 onwards to clear substandard housing and replace it.[9]

We might also find significance in the cost of the building – which was huge. The site accounted for £9,352; the building itself £79,660; and furniture and equipment £26,000.

Equivalencies are always hard to make, but we should remember the building craftsmen who working on the project in 1932 might have earned £3 10s per week. The sources of the money are also indicative of how we should read the story of the building: a combination of miners' welfare fund, borough, and West Yorkshire County Council, backed by collaboration including with the higher education institutions of Leeds and Sheffield. A very tangible expression of the meaning of the cost and origin of the investment comes when we consider that the contribution from the Miners' Welfare of £10,000 towards the building and £5,000 for equipment was funded from a contribution by the coal owners of 1d per ton of coal dug. That contribution to the project was therefore the fruit of the labour which had dug 3.6m tons of coal from the seams around Barnsley.[10]

---

8. Antonia Brodie et al. (eds), *Directory of British Architects, 1834–1914* (London: Continuum, 2001).
9. For more detail on this, see Jayne Dowle's contribution to this volume, at pp. 87–89.
10. John Benson, 'Coalminers, coalowners and collaboration: the miners' permanent relief fund movement in England, 1860–1895', *Labour History Review*, 68 (2003), pp. 181-94; Colin Griffin, 'Not just a case of baths, canteens and rehabilitation centres: the Second World War and the recreational provision of the Miners' Welfare Commission in coalmining communities', in Nick Hayes and Jeff Hill (eds), *'Millions like us'? British Culture in the Second World War* (Liverpool: Liverpool University Press, 1999), pp. 261–94.

We can also read some important tensions and rivalries in the building too. In the same way that there was concern that one had to get far higher marks in the 11+ in Barnsley to get to grammar school than in neighbouring boroughs, so there was a sense that support for mining students discriminated against those from Barnsley – that the scholarships went to Leeds and Sheffield people.[11] The local determination to invest in the new college building was in part a response to what was perceived as many years of poorer treatment: to establish mining education in Barnsley with a status which meant the town was no longer a poor relation of the cities.

What are the contemporary resonances of all this? Since 2005, the University Centre Barnsley, recently renamed University Campus Barnsley, part of the University of Huddersfield, has occupied the spaces opened back in 1932, with its foundation stone laid by Herbert Smith two years previously – what resonances are to be found in this new manifestation for the building?

There are important echoes of some of the major themes we have already seen in the building's history. Something of the spirit of those connections and collaborations can be found in a continuing strong spirit of partnership – a key role has been played by the Barnsley College, Barnsley Metropolitan Borough Council, and important partners in the town such as the *Barnsley Chronicle* newspaper with its proprietors the Hewitts and editor, Robert Cockcroft, Primary Care Trust, hospital, and Rotherham and Barnsley Chamber of Commerce. There is also the same spirit of pride and friendly rivalry, of distinctiveness and yet connection – that we in Barnsley may at times appear to be in the shadow of the big cities, but we and they have much to gain from our determination to stand on our own two feet.

There's also the same ambition to offer an excellent and broad-ranging set of opportunities in education. Just as in earlier years the county borough were always keen that this would not simply be the biggest mining college in the country,

---

11. *Barnsley Chronicle.*

but would also provide a broad range of educational opportunities, so today again students can study across a range of disciplines from computing to art, from humanities to construction, from health to business and from education to journalism.

There are therefore strong continuities to be found in the building: as those who now work there know, so many of the people who come to visit, or to apply and to study, have a connection to the building and to the communities and industries with which it was associated. There is a very strong sense that the men who shifted the tons of coal which paid the pennies into the miners' welfare fund have descendants who can today come into this building in a very different world and benefit from their connection. And those who come here today, and make their contribution through their effort and their fees, are contributing to the building of something even greater for their children.

Those students and staff who have come through the transformation of the building, and those who have observed from outside, know how the accretions of the last fifty years have been stripped out and refurbishment continued. Cutting-edge facilities have been installed to serve all the subject areas, while attempting to remain true to the spirit of the building, providing an evocation of the original building in a modern setting, even down to the detail of the appearance of the 225 windows.

There is also a resonance to be found in the impact to be seen, in growth and the response from local people. At the commencement of the Centre, and its transfer of all existing higher education provision into the Mining and Technical College Building, there were fewer than 400 full-time-equivalent students. In 2007, when the paper version of this chapter was read, the remaining element of that group, the third-year full-time undergraduates, numbered just 47. But as this paper goes to press, there are over 1080 students in higher education at Barnsley, a clear indication of the response from people locally and further afield to the opportunities being developed.

CHAPTER THREE

Mechanics and Miners: The Growth and Development of Adult Education in Barnsley 1831–1964

Martyn A Walker, University of Huddersfield

Historical Overview

1831   First Barnsley Mechanics' Institute founded. Closed within two years.

1834   Second Barnsley Mechanics' Institute founded. Closed after approximately one year.

1837   Third Barnsley Mechanics' Institute founded. Closed by the end of the decade.

1848   The final and permanent Barnsley Mechanics' Institute founded but no purpose-built accommodation.

1830s   Franklin Club Institute opened but closed some twenty years later.

1848   School of Arts and Crafts established.

1877   Mechanics' Institute moves into Eldon Street with additional accommodation in Queen's Road and Hanson Street.

1878   The School of Arts and Crafts moved into the Eldon Street buildings but was not part of the Technical School and Mechanics' Institute.

1889   Technical School, Mechanics' Institute and Library shared accommodation with the Public Hall in Eldon Street which was handed over to the town.

1912   Technical School separated from the Mechanics' Institute, the latter moved into Hanson Street.

1913   Became Barnsley Technical School and School of Arts.

1932   Barnsley Mining and Technical College opened.

1946   School of Arts and Crafts moved into Fairfield House.

*c.*1960 Barnsley Mechanics' Institute in Hanson Street closed.

*c.*1962 The Carr Report highlighted the need to expand Further Education.

1963   Barnsley Mining and Technical College became known as Barnsley College of Technology.

1980s   The former Barnsley Girls' Grammar School became Barnsley College VIth Form Centre.

1990   Barnsley College Old Mill site re-developed. School of Arts and Crafts became part of Barnsley College.

1991   Barnsley Mining and Technical College building re-opened for College courses and the £3.8 million Science Centre was opened.

1997   Eastgate House was added to the Barnsley College campus.

2000   Barnsley College Sixth Form Centre site sold due to a College cash crisis.

2005   Former Barnsley Mining and Technical College buildings purchased by the University of Huddersfield.

Nineteenth-century industrialisation created a need for training and the education of the working class that had previously not been required. In response to the need, mechanics' institutes, providing mainly technical and scientific education for adults, began to spread throughout Britain, starting in 1821 with the establishment of the Anderson Institute in Glasgow. By the mid-eighteen twenties such institutes were to be found in rented buildings or in premises above shops in most parts of Britain. It was, however, common for the institutes to close and re-open during the early years, in some cases several times, as initially they often concentrated on advanced scientific study and public lectures suitable for the already educated (rather than elementary education for the masses), and demand for this was sometimes erratic. Historians have argued that the mechanics' institute movement proved unsuccessful and that it was not relevant to the needs of the working classes. For example,

Kenneth Luckhurst writing in 1957 states that 'Mechanics' institutes ceased to deserve their distinctive name as so few artisans were sufficiently well educated to profit from classes, lectures, libraries and other educational facilities which they provided'.[1] This paper will consider the case of Barnsley.

Early History

The original Barnsley Mechanics' Institute was founded in 1831. Little is known about it but it had a library in premises at the corner of Wellington Street and Pitt Street in the town centre. Classes in elementary education were delivered by Institute staff in the National School in Pitt Street as they had no building of their own. However, this first Barnsley based Institute did not survive for more than a couple of years at best.[2]

A second Barnsley Mechanics' Institute was opened in 1834:

> In the beginning of the year ... a number of young men desirous of improving themselves in useful knowledge met ... and ... commenced a mechanics' institute.[3]

The Committee was made up of a 'druggist', an author, a shoe dealer, a joiner, a warehouseman and two weavers. There were classes in arithmetic, grammar and 'other useful branches of knowledge'. Members paid 1d a week towards the cost of the library.[4]

In the early years of the mechanics' institutes their committees usually included rules preventing religious or political discussions on the premises. In the case of the 1834 Barnsley Institute such regulations were not always adhered to. An Institute member by the name of Crabtree was said to have 'rendered himself notorious as a leader of what was then known

---

1. W. Luckhurst, 'Some Aspects of the History of the Society of Arts' unpublished Ph.D. thesis, (London University, 1957), Chapter X, p.4.
2. Anonymous, *Sketches of Early Barnsley* (Barnsley, 1901), p. 37.
3. *Ibid.*
4. *Ibid.*

as the infidel party [and to have] challenged anyone to prove the existence of a God, or to prove the truths of revealed religion.' The ensuing debate caused a serious split in membership and the result was that both the library and the Institute were sold. Thus, according to the unknown author of *Sketches of Early Barnsley*, 'perished the second attempt to form a mechanics' institute in Barnsley'.[5]

A third Barnsley Mechanics' Institute was established in 1837, and this foundation was to be more permanent. *White's West Riding Dictionary*, published in the same year, stated that the 'Barnsley Institute for promoting education and science by means of mutual instruction, stipendiary teachers, public lectures and a suitable library was established in 1837'.[6] Amongst the founders was Thomas Wilson of Banks Hall, a local colliery owner. During the first year of operation there was a course of lectures given by Professor Simpson of Edinburgh in the same National School, Pitt Street, (which had been used by the 1831 Institute), indicating that the new Institute had no premises of its own. The Institute's library was located next to the Oddfellows (later Temperance) Hall in Pitt Street. Wilson donated books to the library before he and his family moved to Leeds. He had been the first President of the 1837 Institute, and one of the founders of the Yorkshire Union of Mechanics' Institutes. Lucy Wilson, his daughter, would become a promoter of women's education, founding the Leeds Ladies' Educational Association more than thirty years later, in 1869.[7]

Nationally, many mechanics' institutes were established and developed in rented accommodation, most getting their own purpose-built accommodation only after the 1870s. Barnsley was no exception. For nine years the Institute was in 'lodgings', moving from one part of the town to another, including locations on Market Hill.[8]

---

5. *Ibid.*
6. *Ibid.*, p. 38.
7. Peter Gosden, 'Wilson, Lucy (1834-1891)', *Oxford Dictionary of National Biography* (Oxford: Oxford University Press, 2004).
8. *Sketches*, p. 38.

Barnsley also had the Franklin Club Institute, which was thought to have taken some students away from the 1837 Mechanics' Institute, although little is known about its activities. Like the Mechanics' Institute, it was a member of the Yorkshire Union of Mechanics' Institute. This eighteen thirties Club may well have contributed to the closure of the Institute which was, by the end of the decade 'as dead as the proverbial door nail'.[9] In 1848, however, the Mechanics' Institute was re-opened yet again and was to become the basis on which adult education has continued up to the present day.[10] In 1850 the Franklin Club Institute had only 30 members (as compared with 364 who attended the 1848 Barnsley Mechanics' Institute) and thereafter no reference is made to the Club.[11]

It seems the town was keen to provide education opportunities for working-class adults. In 1848, the *Barnsley Chronicle* stated that:

> Barnsley Town stands isolated; therefore to retrieve the character of the town in this respect is the motive to re-establish a mechanics' institute so that people in many places of minor importance are diffusing useful knowledge amongst the young through the mechanics' institute.[12]

The newspaper went on to state that Barnsley was a large manufacturing town of 15,000 people and considered it important that the town should raise its moral standards and its level of intellectual improvement where 'the temptations of vice and dissipation exists in a hundred-fold degree, to the means of advancement'. Apart from encouraging the young males of the town to make more of their lives through education, there was the opportunity for tradesmen, 'where they see the desire for improvement on the part of their assistants', to make use of the Mechanics' Institute classes. Fees of 10 s a quarter were charged to members, which was to prove

8. *Sketches*, p. 38.
9. *Ibid.*
10. *Ibid.*
11. J. W. Hudson, *The History of Adult Education* (1851; reproduced London: Woburn Press, 1969), p. 232.
12. *Barnsley Chronicle*, 28 Mar 1848.

to be too high.[13] In the same year women were admitted to the Institute library and public lectures, and membership rose above 200.[14]

At this stage it is important to set the Barnsley Mechanics' Institute in a national and regional context. In 1838, the Yorkshire Union of Mechanics' Institutes had been formed and Barnsley Institute was one of the first to join. In 1851, Dr J W Hudson published *The History of Adult Education*. His research was based on Britain as a whole, and in the appendices he listed all the mechanics' institutes he knew of by county. Both the 1848 Barnsley Mechanics' Institute and the Barnsley Franklin Club Institute were listed as being members. According to Hudson, in 1850 the Barnsley Mechanics' Institute had 256 members and the Franklin Club Institute had 30. No further reference has been found in relation to the Club Institute and it must be assumed that it closed soon after. The Barnsley Mechanics' Institute charged 1s 6d for three months attendance. It had 1,100 books in its library, and loaned 5,670 books out during 1850, an average of twenty-two books per member. There were 100 pupils attending classes and twenty public lectures had taken place during the year.

In 1850, the Edinburgh Mechanics' Institute had the largest membership of any for the whole of Britain, with 2,035. The Leeds Mechanics' Institute was second with 1,852, Huddersfield Mechanics' Institute tenth and Barnsley Mechanics' Institute 119th, out of 734. Table 1 shows Barnsley Mechanics' Institute's position in relation to membership for the whole country in 1851.

In the Yorkshire Union of Mechanics' Institutes, Barnsley was ranked seventh largest out of 148 in 1851 (see Table 2). There would be, in total 633 institutes belonging to the Yorkshire Union between 1838 and 1900.

Hudson's work indicates that mechanics' institutes were located throughout Britain, with the highest concentrations being found in Yorkshire, Lancashire and in and around the city of Glasgow (see Map 1):

13. *Ibid.*
14. *Ibid.*; Yorkshire Union of Mechanics' Institutes, *Annual Reports.* statistical tables.

Table 1: Rank Order by Membership of some Mechanics' Institutes in Britain.

Position and Institute	No of Members
1. Edinburgh	2,035
2. Leeds	1,852
3. Manchester	1,614
10. Huddersfield	887
11. Bradford	876
72. Oldham	355
82. Sheffield	334
116. Wolverhampton	260
119. Barnsley	**256**
170. Doncaster	200
196. Blackburn	170
547. Rotherham	50

Table from Hudson, *History of Adult Education*, pp. 222–36

In 1848, Barnsley Mechanics' Institute moved location from Wellington Street to Central Chambers in Church Street, with the exception of the main lecture hall, which was located in a former theatre.[15]

In 1876, the Mechanics' Institute at Barnsley remained dispersed across the town with the School of Art, Library, Lecture Hall and News-room all separated from each other. Classrooms in local school were also used for teaching. A new technical school and mechanics' institute building, located in Eldon Street, was opened in January 1878 and included a lecture hall, reading-room, library, museum and classrooms. £16,000 was raised in shares. The building was of Italian style and included accommodation for the hall-keeper.[16]

In October 1878, Barnsley Mechanics' Institute proudly hosted the Forty-First Yorkshire Union of Mechanics' Institutes Conference in the Eldon Street building. There were

15. *Barnsley Chronicle*, 7 Apr 1851.
16. *Barnsley Chronicle*, 4 Oct 1878.

Table 2: Barnsley position in the Yorkshire Union of Mechanics' Institutes: 1850.

1. Leeds	1,852
2. Huddersfield	887
3. Halifax	551
4. York	492
5. Sheffield	390
6. Keighley	300
7. Barnsley	**256**
8. Scarborough	224
9. Skipton	114

Table from Hudson, *History of Adult Education*, pp. 232–34.

Map 1.

representatives from the Clothworkers Company of London, the Science and Art Department at South Kensington, Hull, Leeds, Brighouse, Barnsley, Bradford, Keighley, Wakefield, Garforth, Rotherham, Honley, Mexborough, Heckmondwike, Lower Wortley (Leeds), Ossett, Hebden Bridge, Lockwood, Malton, Knottingley, Lindley, York, Halifax, Lowerhouses, Batley, Castleford, Lofthouse, Middlesbrough, Pudsey, Guiseley, Slaithwaite, Greetland, Hopetown, Scarborough, Wortley (Sheffield), Stanningley, Bramley, Rothwell, Horsforth, Sheffield, Yeadon, Holbeck, Woodhouse, Birstal, Huddersfield, Dewsbury, Stocksbridge, Farsley, Harrogate, Thornton, Cleckheaton, Mirfield, Ilkley, Carlton, Eccleshill, Apperley Bridge, Marske-by-the-sea, Saltaire, Penistone, Hightown, Bingley and Calverley. The main theme of the conference was Art Education and the need to encourage its development in relationship to design and decoration for manufacture. The number of institutes represented gives some indication to the size of the Yorkshire Union.[17]

Relating local population to the membership of each Yorkshire Union Institute over the period 1840–90 indicates that the Barnsley Institute was successful (see Maps 2–5). The ratio also shows that, per head of population, several rural institutes had more members than those found in some expanding towns, indicating that they were successful in offering education to adults.[18]

Population data from census returns and membership statistics from the Yorkshire Union annual returns 1828–1900 provides evidence of many mechanics' institutes in the Yorkshire Union.

---

17. *Barnsley Chronicle*, 4 Oct 1878.
18. For further information in relation to the history of the Yorkshire Union and the debates associated with their development and working-class membership see M. A. Walker, 'A Solid and Practical Education within the Reach of the Humblest Means: The Yorkshire Union of Mechanics' Institutes 1838–1891' (soon to be examined Ph.D. thesis, University of Huddersfield).

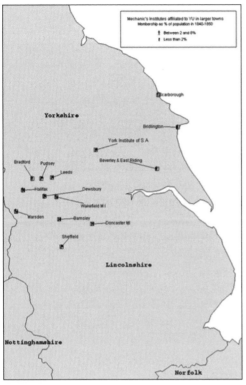

Map 2.

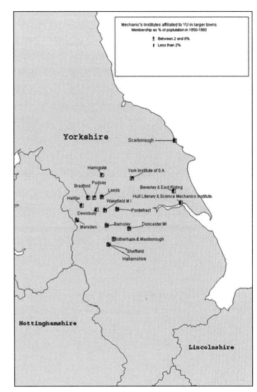

Map 3.

The success of the Barnsley Institute is further emphasised by the fact that its membership over the period 1838–80 overtook the Sheffield Mechanics' Institute founded in the growing and prosperous iron and steel town (Table 3).

Table 3: Mechanics' Institute Memberships at Barnsley and Sheffield.

Institute	1838	1840	1850	1860	1870	1880	1890
Sheffield	352	–	390	300	308	430	–
Barnsley	152	–	256	316	312	576	–

Annual Reports of the Yorkshire Union of Mechanics' Institutes, Statistical Tables.

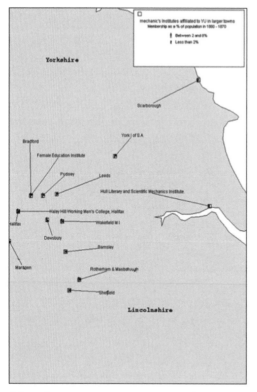

Map 4.

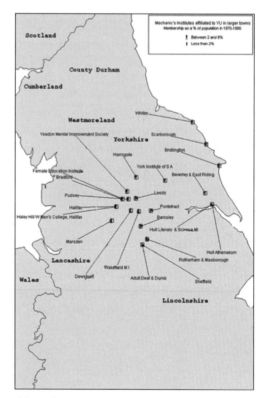

Map 5.

At the same time, women were being encouraged to join institutes and, although membership was relatively small at Barnsley, as elsewhere, females were beginning to take advantage of adult education opportunities.

Table 4: Male and Female Membership sampled over three specific years 1850–80.

Institute	1850			1861			1880		
	Male	Female	Total	Male	Female	Total	Male	Female	Total
Barnsley	219	37	256	267	40	307	506	70	576

Annual Reports of the Yorkshire Union of Mechanics' Institutes, Statistical Tables.

Table 5: The Worshipful Company of Clothworkers, London.

Yorkshire Institutes which received funding	*Date from which funds allocated*
Yorkshire College of Science (later University of Leeds)	1875
Huddersfield Mechanics' Institute (later University of Huddersfield)	1877
Bradford Mechanics' Institute (later University of Bradford)	1878
Barnsley Mechanics' Institute	**1878**
Keighley Mechanics' Institute	1878
Batley Mechanics' Institute	1878
Saltaire Mechanics' Institute	1880
Dewsbury Mechanics' Institute	1883
Halifax Mechanics' Institute	1883
Bingley Mechanics' Institute	1884
Morley Mechanics' Institute	1886
Wakefield Mechanics' Institute	1890
Holmfirth Mechanics' Institute	1893

The Clothworkers' Company, Trusts and General Superintendence Minutes, 1875–1914.

Barnsley Mechanics' Institute was one of several institutes in the North of England that had financial backing from the Worshipful Company of Clothmakers, although there is no evidence as to how much it received.

Examinations
The first nationally recognised examinations to be offered across the country through the mechanics' institutes were those set in 1853 by the Science and Art Department based at South Kensington, London, which became part of the new Education Department in 1856.[19] Society of Arts examinations were

---

19. Helen Sillitoe, *A History of the Teaching of Domestic Subjects* (London: Methuen & Co., 1933), p. xvi.

introduced in 1855, with candidates from mechanics' institutes throughout Britain sitting the exams at the society's headquarters in London. In 1857, Huddersfield Mechanics' Institute became the first centre outside London to administer the society's examinations as it was difficult for candidates to travel to London to undertake assessment over three or four days.[20] The City and Guilds of London Institute for the Advancement of Technical Education was formed in 1884, and their qualifications were offered at mechanics' institutes including the one at Barnsley, by which time a technical school had been attached to the Institute.

Several mechanics' institutes provided university extension scheme classes which gave working-class men, and some women, the opportunity to embark on higher-level courses. They seem to have been established in Lancashire and Yorkshire between 1885 and 1902, and it was often the Co-operative movement that was behind the scheme in towns which had established institutes.

The Cambridge University Extension Scheme was offered at Barnsley (1887), Doncaster, Hebden Bridge, Rotherham, Shipley and Sowerby Bridge. The majority of students were not working men, but some were at Iilkey, Halifax, Cleckheaton, Keighley and Bradford, but some were.[21] Twelve Cambridge University Extension lectures were given at Barnsley in 1887 by W W Watts BA, of the Geological Society, and the first of these, which was free, was attended by the Mayor of the town. This was significant as Watts himself remarked that the University

20. M. A. Walker, 'Examinations for the "Underprivileged" in Victorian Times: the Huddersfield Mechanics' Institution and the Society of Arts, Manufactures and Commerce' (The William Shipley Group for the Royal Society of Arts, 2008), p. 23.

21. N. A. Jepson, *The Beginnings of English University Adult Education: Policy and Problems: A Critical Study of the Early Cambridge and Oxford University Extension Lecture Movements between 1873 and 1907, with Special Reference to Yorkshire* (London: Joseph, 1973), p. 138.

Table 6: List of Mechanics' Institutes in the Yorkshire Union that were part of the University Extension Scheme.

Barnsley	Hartlepool, & West Hartlepool	Pontefract	Sunderland
Bradford	Hebden Bridge	Ripon	Thirsk
Cleckheaton	Heckmondwike	Rotherham	Todmorden
Doncaster	Huddersfield	Scarborough	Whitby
Dewsbury	Hull	Sheffield	York & Railway Institute
Doncaster	Ilkley	Shipley	
Filey	Keighley	Skipton	
Halifax	Leeds	Sowerby Bridge	
Harrogate	Middlesbrough	Stockton	

Jepson, *Beginnings of English University Adult Education*, p.138.

Extension movement had been established nationally to serve towns which had no university but which desired higher education, the students being assessed through questions asked during the lectures. During the remaining eleven weeks, attendees were charged a nominal weekly fee and students gained certificates on completing the examinations successfully. By 1892 there were over fifty Oxford University Extension Scheme centres, with Hebden Bridge, Huddersfield and Ilkley the most established, (but not the only ones) in Yorkshire (Table 6).[22] The Gilchrist Education Trust was set up nationally to fund public lectures on literary and scientific subjects through mechanics' institutes and these were undertaken at Barnsley during 1892.[23] Around the same time a public hall in Eldon Street was being built for general use and incorporated space which could be utilised by all aspects of the Institute under one roof. This included a museum which had a geology section, appropriate in relation to the local coal industry.[24]

22. *Ibid.*
23. *Barnsley Chronicle*, 4 Oct 1892.
24. *Barnsley Chronicle*, 17 Feb 1876.

As late as the eighteen eighties, mechanics' institutes still represented the most important and widespread development in support of working-class adult education. Some new mechanics' institutes had been established during the eighteen seventies and eighteen eighties, especially in the industrial areas.[25] Where there was a demand for skilled and educated workmen, the institutes responded by offering technical education with publicly-recognised examinations through City and Guilds and the Society of Arts. Initially, these activities took place in the North of England. In the South there was less interest in technical education and the institutes tended to be general libraries and scientific societies, with an emphasis on the loan of books, general lectures and social activities rather than on formal classes.[26] The Education Act of 1870 'created a mechanism to provide an elementary school wherever needed', although it did not provide a system of getting children into these schools, once they were built.[27] There is no doubt, however, that the 1870 Act highlighted government intervention in relation to elementary education, the foundation of which was established by mechanics' institutes in the case of the members of the Yorkshire Union at least.

By 1900 the mechanics' institutes were in rapid decline, being replaced by technical schools and colleges. They had served a useful purpose and had been the mainstay during the period from the eighteen fifties to the eighteen eighties when no government support had been available. Local authorities were, however, to take responsibility for technical education

---

25. As late as 1875 both Crewe and Nottingham Mechanics' Institutes played an important part in the inauguration of the University Extension Movement. At Crewe classes were not taken over by the local authority until 1912 and the library not until 1936: Thomas Kelly, *A History of Adult Education in Great Britain* (Liverpool: Liverpool University Press, 1962), p. 199.

26. *Ibid.*, p. 198.

27. Gillian Sutherland, 'Education', in F. M. L. Thompson (ed.), *The Cambridge Social History of Britain, 1750–1950* (3 vols, Cambridge: Cambridge University Press, 1990), iii. 143.

and with the establishment of publicly-funded libraries and museums the end was imminent. Many local authorities not only took over from mechanics' institutes the responsibilities of curriculum and examinations, but also the buildings themselves. Consequently, many mechanics' institutes went on to become technical colleges, such as those in Glasgow, Edinburgh, Manchester, Leeds, Huddersfield, Bradford, Birmingham and Barnsley, and many would later be re-constructed as universities.[28]

Thus, the end of the mechanics' institute was not inglorious. They perished, indeed, for the most part, but they left behind them a legacy of useful public institutions.[29]

Government Involvement

By the late nineteenth century the Government was 'shamed' into taking action. The British exhibits at the Paris Exhibition in 1867 had been sub-standard in comparison to those from other countries. A Parliamentary Select Committee, including Sir Swire Smith of Keighley, and no fewer than two Royal Commissions, resulted in the passing of the Technical Instruction Act of 1889. The *Report of the Royal Commission on Technical Instruction* (The Samuelson Report) had been published in 1884. Bernard Samuelson, the Chairman of the Commission, was a former iron-master and engineer prior to becoming a MP in 1859 and had a personal interest in technical instruction, travelling throughout Europe making comparisons. Swire Smith had been born in Keighley in 1842 and educated at the Wesleyan Voluntary School in the town. At 14 he attended the Wesleyan College in Sheffield and in 1862 set up his own spinning business in Keighley, where he would become president of the town's Mechanics' Institute. Both Samuelson and Smith were aware of foreign competition and wanted technical education to maintain Britain's leading

28. Norman McCord, *British History 1815–1906* (Oxford: Oxford University Press, 1991), p. 348.
29. Kelly, *History of Adult Education*, p. 200.

economic position in the industrial world.[30] Smith visited Belgium to look at technical education there and was concerned that Britain was not keeping up with her competitors. He believed 'effective labour ... was the most powerful weapon with which to meet our wants' and it was to be achieved through technical education.[31] Smith's publication, celebrating the forty-ninth anniversary of the Yorkshire Union in 1886 and, based on findings which were to support the Technical Instruction Act of 1889, identified that operatives in Britain had more leisure time, working 56 hours, compared with those in France, Belgium and Germany who all worked 72 hours. This meant, in Smith's view, that in England night schools could be offered for those who could earn wages during the day and then study in the evening, a tradition of adult learning that was supported by the Technical Instruction Act. The Technical Instruction Act of 1889 empowered local councils to establish Technical Instruction Committees and to charge 1d. rate for the purpose of providing technical and manual instruction. 'Whisky money', tax raised on the sale of whisky, was used to support technical education. By the time the tax ceased in 1902 technical education was well established through central funding from government.[32]

Technical Schools and Mechanics' Institutes

In the early years of the twentieth century, with government funding, mechanics' institutes across Britain became part of the new evolving group of technical schools and, where appropriate, often used former mechanics' institute buildings as part of these developments. At Keighley, for example, the mechanics' institutes became a Trade School for vocational courses in weaving, chemistry, heat and sound, magnetism and elementary education based on the three Rs. By the twentieth century the

---

30. J. Stuart Maclure, *Educational Documents: England and Wales 1816 to the Present* (Methuen, London, 1965, reproduced 1974), p. 121.
31. *Bradford Observer*, 4 Dec 1882.
32. Maclure, *Educational Documents*, p. 198.

building became Keighley College of Further Education.

When the new Huddersfield Mechanics' Institute building was opened in 1878, it was as 'the mechanics' institute and technical school'. It later became the Technical College, and the building is now part of the School of Human and Health Sciences at the University of Huddersfield.

As previously mentioned, the new technical school and mechanics' institute at Barnsley moved into new premises in Eldon Street in January 1877, and into other accommodation in Queen's Road and Hanson Street. Some evening classes were delivered in the elementary schools. Charles Harvey JP funded the Library and technical school and the mechanics' institute all under one roof in Eldon Street. The building, as well as having a public hall, also had shops and offices which would provide additional income generation. In 1889, Harvey handed the Library and Technical School with the Mechanics' Institute to the town.[33]

In September 1912, the Barnsley Mechanics' Institute split from the technical school and moved to Hanson Street with 300 members who enjoyed the opportunity to use the library and

Table 7: Barnsley Technical School Academic Year 1910–11.

Examination	Number of successes
County Council Mining Examinations	45
County Council Science Examinations	45
Board of Education (General) Examinations	7
County Council Commercial Examinations	69
National Union of Teachers' Examination	31
Royal Society of Arts Examinations	17
City and Guilds London Institute (trades)	48
Scholarships to Sheffield and Leeds Universities	9

The Barnsley Education Committee Annual Distribution of Prizes and Report 1912, p. 2.

---

33. Death of Mr Charles Harvey JP, *Barnsley Chronicle*, 5 Nov 1898.

news-rooms. Courses for full and part time students were now the total responsibility of the Technical School in Eldon Street.[34]

Barnsley Technical School and Mining Education

The 1912 Technical School provided a firm foundation on which Barnsley adult education could be further expanded. The West Riding County Council supported the Yorkshire College (later the University of Leeds) and Firth College (later the University of Sheffield), both of which had important mining departments supporting the Technical School at Barnsley before World War One. It was the newly created County Borough Council in the town which encouraged other subjects to be offered. Meanwhile, the West Riding County Council funded six or seven other centres of mining education, including Dinnington, Mexborough and Whitwood.[35] As recently as 1960 most staff at the Barnsley Technical College had degrees in mining and mechanical engineering from the University of Sheffield.[36]

In 1911, the Coal Mines Act included legislation in relation to education and training for employees working in mining. A Central Board for Mining Examinations was established and all employees wishing to enter, or be promoted to, senior posts were expected to gain qualifications in the relevant fields. In 1932, as a direct, if delayed, result of the 1911 Act, Barnsley would have its own purpose-built Mining and Technical College.[37]

In 1912 a *report* was given by D Paton Grubb, the Headmaster of the Barnsley Technical School, which included evening continuation classes delivered at various schools in the town.[38] It highlighted that day courses had been established for men working on shifts in the local industries, including mining and building. Grubb recommended that the Technical School

34. *Barnsley Chronicle*, 28 Sept 1912.
35. P. H. J. H. Gosden and P. R. Sharp, *The Development of an Education Service: The West Riding, 1889–1974* (Oxford: Martin Robertson, 1978), pp. 26–28.
36. *Barnsley College Prospectus 1962–63*.
37. *Barnsley Technical School Magazine*, No.1, Vol. 1 (Jan 1912), p. 5.
38. Grubb would be the first Principal of the new Mining and Technical College in 1932, indicating that he was responsible for Barnsley's technical education for over 20 years. *Barnsley Technical School Magazine*, No.1, Vol. 1 (Jan 1912).

should have its own building and closer links with 'employers of labour'.[39]

The Report indicated that during the academic year 1910–11, there were six academic schools (departments), 40 staff and 910 students at the Technical School. It also provided a summary of examination results (Table 7).

The Technical School, including associated buildings, would be replaced by the Mining and Technical College in 1932.

Barnsley School of Arts and Crafts
Running parallel was the separate Barnsley School of Arts and Crafts. This was established in 1848 and, unlike many mechanics' institutes and technical colleges, which incorporated schools of art, art and craft education was organised and managed separately at Barnsley. The original Art School was above the Post Office in Church Street. In 1860, there was a meeting in a coffee shop in Eldon Street to establish drawing classes. By 1874, school rooms belonging to the Band of Faith Chapel School Churchfield were being used. In 1878, the School of Arts and Crafts moved into the Eldon Street buildings but not under the same management as the Technical School.

By 1925, full-time courses were being offered, and ten years later the School of Art and Crafts was still separate from the Technical College. In 1946, it moved into Fairfield House, being staffed by the Principal (L H H Glover), three full-time and seven part-time staff.[40] The School continued to be independent until 1990 when it merged with the Barnsley College.

Meanwhile, in 1912, Professor Hardwick and Dr Ripper of the University of Sheffield attended a public meeting in Barnsley strongly supporting the implementation of further technical education. During a visit made to the town in 1913, Sir Swire Smith further encouraged Barnsley to develop technical education based on his work abroad. He had been an active supporter of Keighley Mechanics' Institute and Technical

---

39. *The Barnsley Education Committee Annual Distribution of Prizes and Report 1912 of the Technical School and Evening Continuation Schools*, p.1.
40. Barnsley School of Arts and Crafts, *Official Opening of Fairfield House*, p. 9.

School. Thus, both national events and local activities firmly established the idea of extending technical education for all.

The Great War of 1914–18 put many educational developments on hold. At Barnsley, however, the Technical College and Mechanics' Institute needed additional accommodation and further buildings including a former warehouse in Hanson Street.[41] The Technical College and Mechanics' Institute continued to expand its accommodation. The Queen's Road site buildings included 'some corrugated-iron structures adapted for use as a cookery room'. Other parts of the College were located in the Race Common Road, Agnes Road, Worsbro' Common and Burton Road Schools and in the Co-operative guild rooms.[42] In 1924, the West Riding Education Committee agreed to build the Mining and Technical College and during the year architectural plans were drawn up.

The Barnsley Mining and Technical College

In April 1930, the Foundation Stone was laid for the new Mining and Technical College, which was opened on 10th October 1932 by Alderman H M Walker JP.[43] The architects were Briggs and Thornely of Liverpool, and the builder was Charles Smith from Barnsley. The site covered 2,974 square yards and had cost £9,352 to purchase. The building cost £79,660 and furniture and equipment a further £26,000. The Miners' Welfare Fund grant provided £10,000 towards the building and a further £5,000 towards equipment.[44] The remainder of funding came from the County Borough of Barnsley Education Committee.[45] The bricks were made locally at Stairfoot brickworks and were double-pressed so as to make them extremely hard-wearing as well as giving them a decorative appearance. At the same time the Mechanics'

---

41. Ordnance Survey Map of Barnsley, 1:2500, One inch to One mile (1962).
42. *Barnsley Independent*, Oct 1932 (Special supplement celebrating the opening of the Mining and Technical College).
43. *Barnsley Chronicle*, 2 Apr 1930.
44. *Barnsley Independent*, 18 Oct 1932.
45. Opening Ceremony of the New Mining and Technical College Pamphlet, p. 3.

Institute separated from the Technical College and moved into old buildings in Church Street and a former factory before moving permanently into Hanson Street, off Regent Street South. Nothing now remains of the Institute.[46]

The *Barnsley Chronicle* captured the opening ceremony in 1932 with the headline 'The Largest Mining College in the Country'. The paper went on to say that 'Barnsley is the vanguard of striking educational change'. The keynote speaker was Sir Michael Sadler, Master of University College Oxford, who had local connections.[47] He highlighted in his speech that the West Riding Education Committee was deeply interested in the 'new school' for it served not only Barnsley, but also some hundred square miles of South Yorkshire with a total population of 127,000. He stated that 5,100 students were attending junior technical schools and they would potentially feed into the new College.[48]

Other towns had mining colleges, such as Whitwood near Castleford (now part of Wakefield Further Education College) and Wigan (formerly the Wigan and District Mining and Technical College).

The first Principal of the new College, continuing his role from its predecessor, was D Paton Grubb, BSc, MEng, who was also the Head of the Mining Department indicating the importance of mining curriculum. There was also Mechanical Engineering, Electrical Engineering and Chemistry. These areas were also under the responsibility of the Head of the Mining Department. The other Departments were Building Trades, Senior Commercial, Junior Commercial, General Education, Domestic Studies and Arts.[49]

---

46. 1962 Ordnance Survey Map Barnsley, Barnsley Library, Local Archives.
47. Sir Michael Sadler was born in Barnsley, was Professor of History and Education Administration at Victoria University Manchester, Vice Chancellor of the University of Leeds (1911-23) and finally Master of University College, Oxford (1923-34). He died in 1943. Roy Lowe, 'Sadler, Sir Michael Ernest (1861-1943)', *Oxford Dictionary of National Biography*.
48. *Barnsley Chronicle*, 15 Oct 1932.
49. Opening Ceremony of the New Mining and Technical College 1932 Pamphlet, pp. 4–5.

The accommodation layout of the Barnsley Mining and Technical College at the time of its opening in 1932

Layout of the Mining College

Basement	Room	Description
Elementary Mining Laboratory	A1	Equipment to support elementary mining science, with accommodation for 30 students.
Gas Testing Room	A2	Used for the study of caps on various types of safety lamps. Equipment included a large gas tank. The room could be divided into two parts so that one half could be used for examinations for mine managers.
Mine machinery Laboratory	A3 and A4	Ventilation and fan-testing equipment including various forms of air-pressure and air-volume measuring devices, coal-cutting machines, pneumatic picks and drills, haulage and shaft arrangements, care and maintenance of electric and flame safety lamps.
Mechanical Engineering Department	A5	Printing Room with electric printing apparatus for making prints from drawings of various engineering details.
Motor Engineering Workshop	A6	Practical work in motor engineering.
Boiler House	A7	Steam boiler in connection with teaching and mechanical engineering, coal-fired by hand. The room also housed a boiler for heating the building and providing hot water.
Electrical Engineering Department Laboratory	A8	Running machinery equipment with every type of common electric motor and generator.
Mechanical Engineering Laboratory	A9	Steam engine, turbine dynamos, motor generator and compressed air plant.

Mechanical Engineering Workshop	A10	Lathes, drilling machines, grinders, milling machines, benches, saws and gas-fired forge furnace.
Electrical Engineering and Building Department	A11	The room had been adapted to install electric wiring on specially boarded walls and false ceiling for students to be able to wire a room. Equipment for plumbers, gas fitters, pipe bending and oxy-acetylene welding.
Building Department Woodwork Room	A12	Practical carpentry and joinery, wagon building and pattern making.
South corridor		Standard length of 66 and 100 feet marked by bronze plates set in the floor to facilitate the standardisation of surveyors' chains and measurement.

Ground floor

Mechanical Engineering Department	B1	Lecture Room
Mining Department, Surveying and Drawing Office	B2	Instrumentation for both surface and underground surveying.
Mining Department	B3	Preparation Room
Mining Department	B4	Geological Laboratory, study of geology through rock sections, geological mapping and mineralogy.
Advanced Mining Laboratory	B5	Tuition in coal working and analysis in coal, oil and gas. Surface and underground surveying facilities.
Mining Department Classroom	B6	Dual desks and chairs for flexibility in arrangement.
Examinations Hall	B7	
Electrical Engineering	B8	Advanced Electrical Laboratory, equipment included electrical measuring instruments, telephonic and radio apparatus. Photometric Laboratory for measuring candle-power, etc.

Mechanical Engineering	B9	Lecture Room.
Mechanical Engineering	B10	Drawing Office.
Mechanics' Laboratory	B11	Equipment for experiments into the flow of water through orifices and weirs, losses in pipes and bends and elbows. Apparatus for testing of materials, with 30-ton testing machines of a hydraulic type and 10-ton testing machine, wire testing machines, machines for testing bearings, brake pads etc.
Staff Room	B12	
Enquiry Office	B13	

First Floor

Female Student Common Room	C1	
Principal's Office	C2	
General Office and Library	C3	
Locker Room	C4	
Male Student Common Room	C5	
Mining Department	C6	Classroom
Mining Department	C7	Locker Room
Electrical Engineering	C8	Classroom
Electrical Engineering	C9	Classroom
Building Department	C10	Drawing Office
Building Department	C11	Lecture Room
Building Department	C12	Science Laboratory for testing building materials, hydraulic testing, compression testing, beam and cement testing machines.

Second Floor

Pure Science	D1	Chemistry Laboratory
Pure Science	D2	Advanced Chemistry Laboratory
Dark Room	D3	
Preparation Room	D4	
Lecture Room	D5	Accommodation for 60 students
Commercial Department	D6	General Subjects Classroom
Commercial Department	D7	Geography and General Education
Stores Room	D8	
Commercial Department	D9	General Education Studies
Stores Room	D10	
Commercial Department	D11	Typewriter and Office Skills, with 26 modern typewriters, rotary duplication, filing cabinet gramo-phone for teaching typewriting by rhymatic method
Commercial Department	D12	Economic History and Commercial Subjects
Commercial Department	D13	Language and Communication
Commercial Department	D14	Commercial and General Subjects
Commercial Department	D15	Commercial and General Subjects
Pure Science	D16	Physics Laboratory, Heat, Light, Magnetism and Electricity
Roof		Flat roof provided the facility for surveying, lateral studies and azimuth observations. Experimental tanks connected with the hydraulics systems in the Mechanical Engineering Department.

Opening Ceremony, pp. 6–7.

The curriculum offered by the College was established on the traditions of the mechanics' institute and technical school subjects, namely chemistry, physics (heat, light, magnetism and electricity) and local industries, particularly mining.

Floor Plans of the College

Below are the floor plans for the new mining and technical college at Barnsley.[50]

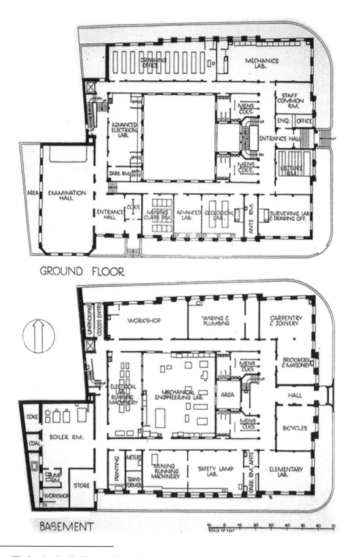

GROUND FLOOR

BASEMENT

---

50. *Technical College Buildings: Their Planning and Equipment'. A Report by the Joint Committee of the Association of Technical Institutions and the Association of Principals of Technical Institutions with Representatives of the Royal Institute of British Architects and*

SECOND FLOOR

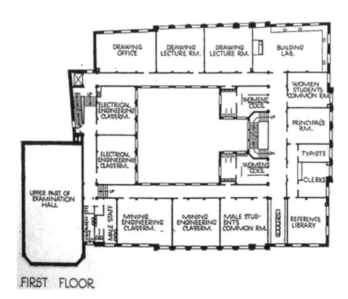

FIRST FLOOR

An inspection was undertaken at the Mining College in 1936 by an HM Inspector on behalf of government. The report provides insight into student numbers and classes being offered.

the Institute of Builders and a Members of the Staff of the Board of Education ([London]: Association of Technical Institutions and Association of Principals of Technical Institutions, 1935), pp. 124–5.

Table 8: Her Majesty's Inspector's External Report carried out at the Mining College in 1936.

Evening Classes	Number of Students
Mechanical Engineering	199
Electrical Engineering	136
Science	44
Domestic Studies (Needlework and Dressmaking)	256
Part-time Day Classes	
Mechanical and Electrical Engineering	59
Science	35
Domestic Studies	74

Full-time Classes	
Science and Engineering	57
Domestic Studies	31
Other subject areas inspected	No data
Chemical Industries and Fuel Course	No data
Paper Manufacturing	No data
Bakery and Confectionary	No data
Glass-making	No data
Higher (education) Work	No data

His Majesty's Inspectors of Schools, *Inspection Report for 1936 Barnsley Mining College*, pp. 4–5.

The inspectors found 'work as a whole is good and thorough and thoroughly planned'. Students were, however, perceived not to bring enough initiative and enterprise to their studies, but to:

Follow in a docile manner the path prepared for them ... students need more stimulus, partly due to the drab surrounding of the town and mining villages and the economics practiced with regard to books, periodicals, illustrations and materials.[51]

---

51. *HMI Inspection Report for 1936 Barnsley Mining College*, p. 6.

The *Report* made several recommendations. Heating in some of the classrooms was unsatisfactory. The Head of Department for Mining, who oversaw all subjects and departments, 'should have a private room' and there ought to be the 'appointment of a full-time teacher and competent laboratory steward'.[52]

Other recommendations included development of higher-level work, the appointment of a full-time teacher in science and engineering, that the motor car engine course should be reviewed, that the annual allowance for all departments should be increased and that there should be an appointment of a laboratory assistant for electrical engineering.

The Government White Paper on Technical Education, the Carr Report of 1962, stressed that there should be a fifty per cent increase in students for advanced courses at technical colleges and the need to double the numbers needing support from employers in relation to 'low-level part-time courses during the day'.[53] The Carr Committee had identified the number of fifteen-year-olds rising from 640,000 in 1956 to

Table 9: Salaries in the mining industry in relation to qualifications 1962.

Department (Administration)	£18–£20 per week
Under Manager	£1,125–£1,500 p.a.
Manager	£1,400–2,100 p.a.
Agent	£1,750–£2,400 p.a.
Group Manager	£2,000–£2,750 p.a.
Production Manager	£2,250–£3,000 p.a.
Area Manager	£4,000 maximum p.a.
Colliery Engineer	£900–£1,400 p.a.
Group Engineer	£1,005–£1,600
Area Engineer	£1,550–£2,150
Divisional Engineer	£2,000–£2,750

The NCB also sponsored scholarships to University.

Guide to Courses available at Barnsley College of Technology (1962) p. 7.

---

52. *Ibid.*
53. *Guide to Courses available at Barnsley College of Technology* (1963), p. 2.

712,000 in 1958, and estimated to be 929,000 in 1962. With the end of National Service there were between 200,000 to 250,000 young men available for civilian employment and therefore the need for training was a high priority.[54]

The National Coal Board (the coal industry was nationalised in 1946) sponsored mining employees to attend the courses at the College and within the 1962 *Prospectus* provided a salary table in relation to managerial posts in the industry (Table 9). This marketing style was presumably to inspire men to take mining qualifications to support salary increases after promotion in the industry.

In 1962, the College had six departments, the Department of Mechanical Engineering, the Department of Electrical Engineering, the Department of Building, the Department of Commerce and General Education, the Department of Science, and the Department of Household Science and Needlework. By 1964, in addition to the former Mining College building in Church Street, there were two Barnsley College buildings on Old Mill Lane, one at Belle Vue, Longcar Central School and Barnsley Grammar School.[55]

Conclusion

This paper has outlined the growth and development of adult education in Barnsley from 1832. The establishment of a mechanics' institute by enthusiastic young men of working-class origins who wanted to improve their knowledge laid the foundation for adult education. Despite early vulnerability and closure, a Mechanics' Institute finally became permanently established in 1848. The support from the town for the education of tradesmen and particularly that from the local newspaper, *The Barnsley Chronicle*, increased Barnsley Mechanics' Institute's profile. Females were also encouraged to join. The result was that the Mechanics' Institute became successful and was one of over 600 that were part of the Yorkshire Union of Mechanics' Institutes. The poor quality of

54. *Guide to Courses*, p. 6.
55. *Barnsley College of Technology Prospectus 1963–1964*, p. 1.

British industrial exhibits at Paris in 1867 resulted in government taking a more active role in the development of adult education, and the Technical Instruction Act of 1889 empowered local authorities to fund technical schools, the forerunners of colleges. The construction of the Technical School, Mechanics' Institute and Public Hall, the building known as the Harvey Institute, permanently established state-funded technical education in Barnsley to meet the growing need to train employees locally, particularly in the mining industry after World War One. With support from the Local Authority and the Miners' Welfare Fund, the purpose-built Mining and Technical College was opened in 1932, and since then further and higher education in Barnsley has gone from strength to strength.

Postscript
During the 1980s, Barnsley College acquired the town's former Girls' Grammar School, which became the VIth Form Centre, only to be sold in 2000 due to a College cash crisis. In 1990, the Old Mill site was re-developed, and the following year, 1991, the former Mining and Technical College building was re-opened for courses. In the same year a £3.8 million Science Centre was opened, followed by Eastgate House being added to the campus in 1997. In 2005, the former Mining and Technical College was bought by the University of Huddersfield and refurbished, being officially opened as University Centre Barnsley by the Rt. Hon. David Blunkett MP, a former Secretary of State for Education and Skills, a PGCE student of the University of Huddersfield and former lecturer in the business department at Barnsley College. In January 2005, almost £2million were spent on a new Construction and Engineering Centre for Barnsley College on the Old Mill Lane site.[56] In October 2007, the University Centre Barnsley celebrated the 75 years since the opening of the Mining College with a series of lectures and events, including a presentation of this paper.

---

56. *Barnsley Chronicle*, various press cuttings.

CHAPTER FOUR

The Voices in the Stone

Lynn Rollin, University Campus Barnsley

Without the ability to create memories we would perceive no more than each disjointed second of our own isolated existences; we would have no language, no alphabet, no discourse, no identity and no culture ...[1]

How we remember or recollect is uniquely personal. Over time our memories of certain events in our lives fade, become less accurate but the essence remains. Usually the strongest memories are of events or times in our lives, which are significant. They stand out for a variety of reasons. They may be happy memories, a wedding, holidays, the birth of a child, our graduation – or sad, the death of a family member or friend, or an incident that shocked us. Horrific world events are easily recalled. Single words or figures such as 9/11, the Tsunami, are enough to trigger memory. Instantly we remember words, headlines, images that we saw at the time. Significant people and places remain clear in our memory. These could be people who have helped shape our lives in some way, inspired us or made us smile, or places where important events have taken place. We recall these memories in conversation with our friends and family and relate stories from our past that we know will amuse or enlighten others. This story telling is fundamental to our lives. As children we listened enthralled to stories of our parents' early lives and through these

1. B. Brown, 'Typography and artificial memory', in M. Gorman, *Typography New Era New Language: An International Conference on the Teaching and Practice of Typography* (Manchester: Righton Press, 1995), p. 71.

gained understanding and built up images of our historical past. The building in Church Street that is now The University Centre is part of the historical past of the people of Barnsley. Many of them, or members of their family or friends, worked there or studied there. The exhibition 'Voices in the Stone' gives insight into these peoples' lives and their experiences.

Historian Professor Tim Thornton conceived the initial idea. At the opening of the new University Centre Barnsley in 2005 Professor Thornton, then Head of the Centre noticed the date of the original opening of the building. On 10 October 1932 Alderman Henry Mike Walker JP, Chairman of the Higher Education Committee, had opened the building as the Barnsley Mining and Technical College. Professor Thornton realised that the seventy-fifth anniversary was imminent and saw what 'an excellent conjunction' there was between that and the rebirth of the building as The University Centre. He felt that this provided the ideal opportunity to celebrate the achievements of past and present students and staff. Professor Thornton firmly believed that the new University Centre should be seen as 'a rediscovery, a rejuvenation of a strong local pride in education and community rather than something 'new' and 'different' being offered.' He wanted to do something that acknowledged this rejuvenation and strong local pride. In order to accomplish this he applied for and was successful in obtaining an Arts Council Grant in 2006.

The original grant application was for a photographer and writer to produce work in response to the major refurbishment of the building, originally designed by the architect Sir Arnold Thornely and now The University Centre Barnsley. As the building was already in use, the transformation was not simply that of physical space but of the way in which it was used and the communities using it.

In the original grant application it was stated: 'We believe the refurbishment should be refurbishment of the meaning of the building and its role in delivering top-quality education to the people of Barnsley, South Yorkshire, and beyond – not just a refurbishment of bricks and mortar. The resident artists will produce work in response to the work, by being present during refurbishment, interacting with past, current and potential future students'. And also: 'Our objective is to expand dramatically the range and quality of H.E. available to people in this area, making excellence genuinely accessible to all.'

It was felt that the building that was now the new University Centre was a 'landmark' building and that the refurbishment and the transformation of the work of the Centre was something that would spark interest in the local community. Many people had passed through and given the nature of the local community that it was unlikely that many families would have been entirely untouched by its influence at some point in the past.

During the refurbishment Professor Thornton took on a new role as Dean of Music, Humanities and Media and Dr Cathy Doggett became the new Head of Centre and took over the project. The refurbishment was almost complete by the time Dr Doggett was in post and in a position to proceed with the project, and so it was decided to focus more on individuals and their stories. Tenders were invited from both photographers and writers through both local and national advertising. In March 2007 five photographers and five writers were short listed and interviewed. Christopher Sedgewick, photographer, and Jessica Penrose, writer, were successful and became Artists in Residence for the duration of the project.

During a series of meetings between Centre staff, Chris and Jessica, it was decided that an exhibition would be mounted which would contain photographic pieces linked by creative writing, either poetry or prose. The brief was very open and Jessica and Chris set out to find and then interview and photograph past and present students and staff in order to gain insight into their experiences and aspirations, in short to tell their stories. At this stage the project did not have a name but in an early meeting a colleague, Garry Sykes, in a moment of inspiration, suggested 'Voices in the Stone'. This was met with unanimous approval. It was felt that this title evoked images of the many people who had passed through the building and of how they had perhaps influenced and helped to shape the lives of future generations and the future use of the building. It seemed to convey a sense of history and our dependence on each other. Throughout history, artists and writers have been telling stories through their work, some gaining more notoriety and celebrity status than others. Tracey Emin confronts us with her imagery, with her personal story. Her work is so intensely personal that the viewer becomes a voyeur as she confesses through her artwork. For example the installation *My Bed* which is based on her own bedroom is literally an unmade bed with all the detritus of daily life, including dirty underwear, empty bottles and overflowing ashtrays, or the igloo shaped tent provocatively entitled *Everyone I have ever slept with 1963–1995*. This is embroidered on the inside with the names of everyone Emin had slept with and includes her twin brother in the womb, her parents, friends and lovers. By looking we assume an intimacy and knowledge that we find uncomfortable. Paula Rego's work is similarly autobiographical but also a commentary on culture, history and society in her birthplace Portugal. Her paintings are complex with layers of meaning. The messages they contain are subtle, hidden and hard to unravel.

In her graphic work, as in her painting, Rego is a great storyteller who both persuasively and subversively seizes you at the first encounter, and then keeps a relentless grip on your mind and senses until she has finished her complex, infinitely subtle and reverberating tales.[2]

Photographers too tell stories through their work. Richard Billingham's photographs of his family are shocking but also humorous. Billingham started taking photographs of his family as reference material for his paintings but in the nineteen nineties they became critically acclaimed in their own right. They are unlike any photographs one might see in a photograph album as they feature his alcoholic father Ray and his overweight and chain-smoking mother. They highlight their dysfunctional family life and show the poverty and chaos in which they lived. In his work, Martin Parr, documentary photographer and a photojournalist, takes a critical look at modern society, for

---

2. T. G. Rosenthal, cited in P. Coldwell, *Paula Rego Printmaker* (London: Marlborough Graphics, 2005), p. 11.

example the British on holiday in the nineteen eighties. Families are photographed on the beach sitting next to piles of rubbish. His photographs leave the viewer unsure as whether to laugh or to cry. From Jacques-Henri Lartigue we get a glimpse of the lives of the rich and famous. The work which artists produce is by necessity from their own perspective and the photographs produced by Christopher Sedgewick, the photographer engaged to work on 'Voices in the Stone', will be no exception. Chris has a particular empathy with the people of Barnsley as he was born and brought up here. He is a 'Barnsley lad'. Many of his relatives had worked as miners or are the sons and daughters of miners. Chris wanted the images he produced to evoke in others the empathy that he himself feels for the people of Barnsley.

Writers can engage us with long and complex narratives but short stories can be equally compelling. The *Today* programme on Radio Four (2008) reported a story about the writer Ernest Hemingway. In the nineteen twenties Hemingway apparently won a bet for ten dollars by proving that he could write a story in just six words. His story: 'For sale: Baby shoes, never worn.' These few words are enough to allow the reader to speculate and to give their own interpretation of what might have happened. According to the *Today* programme, an American online magazine used this to inspire readers to describe their lives in just six words. Two memorable examples are 'I wasn't born a red head'. And 'Not quite what I had planned'.[3] These examples show how very few words can give us insight and information. Jessica faced a similar challenge.

Jessica and Chris managed to make contact with many people who had spent time in the Church Street building in its various guises. They met with older people who had studied there many years ago whilst still at school, with former miners who went on 'day release' from their job or to night classes, with former Barnsley College lecturers and students as well as present and past students from the University Centre. All were photographed and interviewed. A network of people, including

---

3. The Today programme (2008) BBC Radio 4.

the writer Mel Dyke, passed on personal contacts. Without exception everyone approached was happy to give up their time in order to tell their story. The Mining Museum near Wakefield also proved an excellent source of reference. This process was time consuming and painstaking. In an interview Chris explained that both he and Jessica had gone together to meet with people and that this had proved very successful. Many of the subjects forgot they were being photographed as they told Jessica of their experiences.

Others chatted more generally about their lives and told Chris some amusing anecdotes. For example the miner, Ian Thomas, who broke his leg and was off work for quite a while. Ian lived in a house in the pit yard at Woolley. Every day his work mates knocked him up 'just for a laugh.' Angela Knowles studied secretarial skills at the college and is the subject of one of the photographs. She was 'Miss February' in the risqué and hugely acclaimed Woman's Institute calendar. The calendar, inspired by her, was produced in order to raise money for Leukaemia research after her husband died from the disease at age fifty-four.

Chris explained how he had composed the photographs. Most read from left to right and many contain other elements that give more information about the subjects. These could be mining implements, helmets, protective clothing or in Don Parkin's case his beloved pigeons, captured frozen and surreal in flight. Where possible, Chris photographed his subjects in their own homes or in familiar work related surroundings. Jean Taylor is photographed with a photograph of her father who was a lecturer at the college. She came to the college for tuition in home skills when she was just thirteen and still at school. Gillian Gough who is a recent graduate from the Interdisciplinary Art and Design course at the University Centre strikes a dramatic pose next to the huge breast of one of her sculptures, whilst Mel Dyke looks delighted as she is photographed in her book-lined study.

Some of the larger images are in black and white, some full colour and others have just one element in colour. For example the beautiful yellow sunflowers in the black and white photograph of Angela Knowles are the only part of the image in colour and so are used with dramatic effect. Chris used many photographs on a much smaller scale, placing them in long strips with three or four next to each other. This enabled many more of the photographs to be used alongside the larger images and gave further insight into the lives of the people photographed. These smaller images echo the format of the graphic panels containing the text.

Jessica had the complex task of editing the information that she had obtained. This proved quite challenging as there was so much, all of which gave fascinating insight into the lives of the subjects and their links with the building. It was decided to pick out significant words and phrases to get a collective feeling of peoples' experiences. These were presented in a graphic way, using type as both word and image. Laura Grange, then a final year student on the BA (Hons) Interdisciplinary Art and Design Course at the University Centre, worked with Jessica and Lynn Rollin (Senior Lecturer) in the production of these panels, all of which utilise similar typefaces and formats. Jessica also wished to express the Barnsley accent and dialect as she felt this would give a warmth and directness to the stories she was told. She wanted to try and reproduce it when written in order to give a sense of the person speaking but did not want to compromise legibility. The result is sometimes slightly awkward to read but it is an attempt to fairly represent the spoken word. Short paragraphs from stories told by different people are used on the graphic panels alongside typographic interpretations of these to illustrate the story being told. Using type as image in this way brings out key elements of the story. Some of the stories chosen are amusing, others more poignant. All help us to build up a picture of the lives of the people who have passed through this building and also paint a broader picture of what it was like to live in Barnsley at that time.

We learn of peoples' dreams and aspirations, of the difficulties they had in overcoming obstacles, of the fun they had and of their triumphs and determination. There was Fred Isherwood who smoked a pipe and would put it in his pocket still smoldering. 'Excuse me Fred; I think you're on fire!' A lecturer who taught Mining Industries Basic Skills to a challenging group of students is quoted as saying; 'If you could tackle them you were made for life. You were like a lion tamer, going in with whip and chain. I once went into the classroom and all the tables were on their sides and lads behind them like barricades, throwing pies at each other. Mayhem.'

We learn of women who had left school at fifteen and then gone back into education years later. 'A light would go on in them and they'd want to make a new start.' Although some didn't make it, 'Others stuck it out despite it all, told their men to get their own meals, walked out if that's what it took.' And on results day: 'I never thought I'd do it!'

A student who wants to be a music teacher said, 'I want to take on those kids who'll come out with nothing – open them up. Get them believing in something. After all, three chords and you can be master of the universe.'

One girl hated the aerobics session that took place on Wednesday afternoon. 'Us girls in leotards bending and stretching – every window framed a miner's ogling face'.

Physical training in the big hall consisted of running backwards and forwards, as there was no equipment. One lad put his hand out to stop and turn and managed to put his hand straight through a window reinforced with wire. He trapped his hand and cut an artery. 'Blood were pumping out – it were unbelievable. I grabbed him straightaway and someone had to break glass piece by piece to get him out.'

Any of these stories could strike a chord with any one of us. They are universal and yet very personal at the same time.

As their research progressed final choices of photographs and text were made and it became clear how the exhibition should be mounted. In order to give as comprehensive a picture as possible of the seventy-five year history of the building it was decided that a series of smaller graphic and photographic panels would be placed alongside the larger photographic images. The larger images would have immediate impact but the viewer would have to engage on a much more intimate level with the smaller pieces in order to understand and appreciate the prose. Jessica felt that this intimacy was very important, as these were personal stories. For the same reason none of the quotes are attributed to individuals, only the large photographs bear the person's name.

Many people were involved in mounting the exhibition; it was truly a group effort. Richard Turner and Chris Charlesworth provided technical support, office staff from the University Centre provided administrative support and many colleagues offered their help and advice. The exhibition starts in the entrance foyer of the University Centre and continues up the stairs and around the third floor. The private viewing took place on 10 October 2007 and marked the seventy-fifth anniversary of the opening of the building. All who attended, including some of the people who are represented in the exhibition, were generous in their praise and recognized the quality of the work produced by Jessica and Chris. They have captured the spirit of the people of Barnsley, shown their determination to succeed, their humour and their community spirit.

'Voices in the Stone' is a celebration of the achievements of past and present students and staff. It is testimony to a strong local pride in education and community and an acknowledgement of the rebirth of the building as The University Centre Barnsley.

CHAPTER FIVE

Concept and Creation: The Composition of 'Voices' for Male Voice Choir

Pete Birkby, University Campus Barnsley

When the 'Voices in the Stone' project was first publicised, my immediate thoughts were about music that would complement the text and photographs. I have always held the belief that a composer should be involved with every aspect of the community, not just the traditional festivals; religious or seasonal and general celebrations, and also special events. This has inspired me to write music for events as diverse as amateur sports club presentation evenings, ensemble rehearsals, promotional films and professional concerts and recordings, and 'Voices in the Stone' was immediately appealing as the catalyst for a new composition.

From leading my first band in the late nineteen sixties, I knew that the composer and arranger had one of the most important jobs in music, to facilitate a stimulating and fulfilling experience for musicians and audience alike. To me, the interaction between the performer (including the composer) and the audience is an integral part of most successful musical experiences and one that is sometimes overlooked by some of the participants. That first band played Big Band hits from the nineteen forties with a line-up of trumpet, trombone, clarinet, guitar, piano and a drum (sometimes violin, cello and flute as well) as we tried to recreate the Glen Miller sound as faithfully as we could with our limited resources, carefully sharing out the main themes and solos to a steady groove. The band had some success at school concerts and church fetes and for me as the arranger and sometimes composer that was it: I had started to find ways to make the music work for the forces available. A composing and arranging career seemed the natural progression for a naive fourteen-year-old, and I subsequently joined many other bands and groups and tried out my compositions and arrangements with them. Thanks are due to the many conductors and performers for their patience and support over the years. They were subjected to my first efforts and gave them the same serious consideration and effort as if they were the work of an established professional.

During the weeks after I had heard about the project I had many ideas about the music that would capture the essence of the history, toil and success of the work that had been taught and studied in the building, the ethos of the Church Street site. Where and how the first ideas for a composition appear is still a mystery. Stravinsky wrote about chance and accident, and Mozart, Beethoven and Brahms all wrote about inspiration from God which came to them during the time of semi-consciousness. Much of the musical material I used in 'Voices' materialised in the semi-conscious time, usually just before sleep.

My mind organises ideas into sounds, textures and themes, sometimes with harmony, and capturing these thoughts is a necessity. This is the time for a notebook or some recording device (usually a Dictaphone) to make sure I have some representation of these ideas from the semi-conscious state. These ideas are then tested the next day when wide awake to see if they are still interesting, then refined, edited or discarded before starting the far more time-consuming process of realising the music and/or sounds for performers and/or audience. Some ideas from the semi-conscious state are not fully discarded and may sit in the 'to be considered' file for many months until an appropriate realisation can be formulated.

One of these ideas was to try and include musical influences that spanned the 75 years of the building's existence. The main popular recording artists of 1932 were Louis Armstrong, Bing Crosby, Rudy Vallee, Paul Robeson, Billy Cotton, Al Bowlly, Jeanette MacDonald, Noel Coward, Fred Astaire and Duke Ellington, with *Night and Day* (Cole Porter) and *All of Me*

Angela Knowles. Former student in secretarial skills at the Mining and Technical College. Also Miss February in the Women's Institute Calendar that shot to fame when a film was made of the story behind it, 'Calendar Girls'. Photography Chris Sedgewick

Cllr Bill Newman. Former lecturer at the Mining and Techincal College. Now local councillor representing the Royston Ward and Cabinet Spokesperson for Development. Photography Chris Sedgewick

Dave Halstead. Former mining student in the days of the Mining and Technical College. Photography Chris Sedgewick

Dave Mapson BA (Hons) Popular Music Graduate 2008 at the refurbished buidling – University Campus Barnsley.
Part of the University of Huddersfield. Photography Chris Sedgewick

David Gale. Former mining student in the days of the Mining and Techincal College.
Photography Chris Sedgewick

Don Parkin. Former mining student in the days of the Mining and Techincal College.
Photography Chris Sedgewick

Gillian Gough BA (Hons) Interdisciplinary Art and Design 2007 Graduate. One of the first graduates at the refurbished building – University Campus Barnsley. Photography Chris Sedgewick

Ian Thomas. Former mining student in the days of the Mining and Technical College. Photography Chris Sedgewick

Jean Taylor undertook tuition in home skills at the Mining and Technical College as a 13-year-old and still at school. Photography Chris Sedgewick

Ken Francis. Former mining student in the days of the Mining and Technical College. Photography Chris Sedgewick

Mel Reed. Former student in the days of the Mining and Technical College.
Photography Chris Sedgewick

Mel Dyke, local authoress and historian. Photography Chris Sedgewick

(Seymour Simons) being the biggest selling records of the year. Sergei Prokofiev and Jean Françaix both premiered piano concertos during 1932, Dmitri Kabalevsky his first symphony, Percy Grainger completed *Handel in the Strand* and the virtuoso violinist Jascha Heifetz arranged *Hora Staccato.* Some of the musical films from this year were: *Girl Crazy* with Dorothy Lee, Robert Quillan, Mitzi Green and Kitty Kelly, *Looking on the Bright Side* starring Gracie Fields and *Love Me Tonight* with Maurice Chevalier and Jeanette MacDonald. In the theatre the most popular productions were revues, with Nöel Coward as one of the most popular composer/performers. This concept has remained very popular to the present day but now in the *Songs from the Shows* format.

I already had many years experience of the music from the nineteen thirties, nineteen forties and nineteen fifties, performing as the percussionist with the Max Jaffa orchestra at the Spa in Scarborough. My experience as performer, arranger, composer and listener included most music from the nineteen sixties to the present day. My main influences and experiences from British music are Benjamin Britten, The Who, Brian Eno and James Macmillan, with the transatlantic influences of Duke Ellington, George Gershwin, Frank Zappa and Salsa Music. These many musical styles eventually influenced my own inspiration to create the sound of 'Voices'.

One other idea that was competing for my consideration was to use the sounds made during the refurbishment of the building, the incessant and mostly percussive noises of demolition and construction, to create sounds to be organised into a composition. Eventually I rejected this idea as the sounds of drilling and the occasional sledgehammer would not convey the true spirit and history of the building.

The very first ideas for this composition were melodies (Bar 82); the major/ minor phrases gave me the option to choose positive or critical lyrical material when the transcripts of the interviews from past and current student arrived.

When deciding on the sounds to be used for the composition I felt I had to give prominence to the content of the interviews but also create an idea of the sound in the building – 7.30 in the morning the sounds of preparation for the day, the sound of footsteps and chatter during the rush for food at lunchtime and the more muted sounds of the evening when many part-time students use the Centre. A choir sound was eventually chosen, to give the contrast of high to low voices as well as experimenting with spoken sounds. When the transcripts of the interviews started to arrive there were positive and negative comments from the students and staff that had worked in the building: they either loved or hated being at 'tech'. Jessica Penrose, the creative writer, had also highlighted interesting words relating to the subjects being studied, and these inspired the contrasting whispered elements in the final work (Bar 21).

The final elements to the composition were the introduction of the title of the project, *Voices in the Stone*:

and a fanfare section to herald a new beginning as the University Centre (Bar 35):

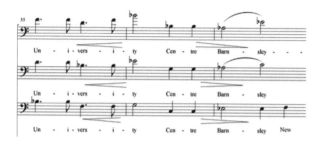

The main musical ideas had been completed, and I considered various combinations of ideas in my mind. These ideas were ordered to create an overall shape to the structure of the music, and then more music was composed to facilitate a flow between the main sections.

Another consideration was the audience and how they would listen to the music. These thoughts led me to compose two versions of the music, one the concert version, the other to be played for people viewing the exhibition. The impression I wanted to create for the audience listening to the concert version was of standing on the main staircase of the building and listening to the gentle cacophony of sounds from various conversations, footsteps in the corridors, and sounds of lectures and discussions behind closed doors. To create some of this effect I took phrases from one interview and placed them after a phrase from a different interview. This effect is repeated throughout the composition with some contrasting sections of short narrative passages or rhythmic whispering with foot tapping. The phrases are also given to various voices in the ensemble, at different volumes, to create a sense of an overheard conversation in the distance.

The exhibition music has some words or phrases from the original recorded interviews mixed in with the musical composition. These phrases have been kept very short and have periods of silence between them. This is to be played during the exhibition and gives a random impression of the voices from the photographs. The loop for the sounds is over thirty minutes long so the viewer in a gallery should not hear the sound repeat.

The melodic idea for the line 'The Voices in the Stone' was influenced by the recordings of Peter Peers and Benjamin Britten that I had heard during the nineteen seventies, the leap of the voice and the intervals Britten used for the compositions and arrangements having been filed away for many years in my memory, only now to be used. The harmony used to accompany the melody also had to create the effect of movement; the composition has a basis in F (major or minor) (chosen as the lowest comfortable note for the bass voice to sing), but Db, D and Eb also feature as tonal centres. The overall structure was already organised and then the lyrical content was added to the various sections of music. With the ideas all complete, the first drafts of the composition were written by hand on manuscript paper and as sections were finalised they were transferred, ready for printing, to music desktop publishing software, which allows for easier editing of the spacing and for the words and syllables in the lyrics to be obviously linked to the music notes. This was very necessary if the composition was to be performed by a choir and the manuscript sets produced for rehearsal and concert. Some test recordings of small sections of the composition were completed at this time to confirm the sound texture was as envisaged.

Computer software can help give an impression or basic realisation of composition but I have used sequencing, recording and notation software for many years and the more developments there are in the software, the more predictive or full of extras (presets, sample loops, sound limitations to the instrument they are emulating, arpeggiators, groove makers, and so on), the more they stifle creativity and inspiration. Many computer users spend little time on considering the musical material but hours on speculatively trawling through banks of sounds and textures in an effort to find some sound that is inspirational. All this effort either leads the user to a mostly predetermined result or the user spends so much time and energy on setting up the program that when it is finally ready there is little or no energy left to be creative. This is why I always complete the main elements of the composition, sounds and instrumentation, textures, tempo, duration, structure and harmony, on paper, either manuscript, graphically or as written descriptions, before turning on the computer.

A major constraint of studio processing and editing is time. To edit, tune-up, correct the rhythm or alter parts of the performance takes a great deal of time and can even run into days. To ask the performer to repeat a performance but to consider some of the aspects that are not exactly as the composer imagined gives instant results and options to cut between a few versions of the same piece of music and to use the best extracts from each. This may seem like deception on the part of both the performer and the recording engineer or producer but a recording can be in the public domain for many years, is often listened to in an individual environment with little distractions, and is a representation of that performer at that time which captures the essence at the time but may not be the complete picture.

Compare this with the 'one off' or never-to-be-repeated live performance which is influenced by the interaction between performer and audience, the environment (sound, heat, other musicians), and the attitudes of the performer and audience.

To complete the recording of the music I tried to create a sense of the space within the building and complement that with a choral performance. Footsteps were used to create an impression of the corridors/ staircase in the final composition to accompany the whispered lyrics. The footsteps were recorded outside the Learning Resource Centre, with size 12 shoes, on the laminate floor and using the Soundfield microphone, on stereo not surround setting, to give the impression of movement across the stereo image in the recording. These footsteps were then edited to a specific tempo, or steps per minute, to become a guide track.

Some test recordings were then taken of the whispering voices and separate recordings of the singing voices. The individual vocal parts were recorded three or four times to build up the sound of a larger choir. At this stage the texture and full sound of over thirty vocalists was not complete. The whispering sections were effective enough but the contrast with the sung parts was not evident. To add more body to the sung sections I doubled up the choir with a background of synthesised choir (of 'oos' or 'ahs') and the real choir was digitally placed in a large hall.[1]

---

1. If a sound is recorded in a controlled environment, without any room sound or *dry*, then it is quite straightforward to use the recording studio software to place the sound in different sized 'rooms' for different echoes or reverberation [wet] effects.

A version was ready but the dialect was not coherent throughout the recording. Some phonetic ideas of the sounds were tried to help the singers create the complete effect of the words with the music, but many of these sounds proved to be very difficult to sing with accurate rhythm and pitch. In the end the dialect was not used as it took away from the final effect of a celebration of the building; the dialect could have become the focal point in the composition but a mix of phrases and voices was the effect I was trying to create.

Throughout the years, the subjects studied in the Church Street building have changed considerably, mining and typing in the early years, popular music, art, business and early years education, to name but a few today, but the sounds of the day have remained similar over the seventy-five years. I hope my composition adds to the legacy of the building. It is the first composition I have written that has been so influenced by one environment. The sounds inside the Centre are still constantly changing; there are still students that love it or hate it, and I hope it will serve the people of Barnsley for another seventy-five years.

Included below is the score to *Voices,* used by kind permission of Peter R Birkby Publishing.

Voices
For Male Voice Choir
Composed to Celebrate 75 Years of the Church Street Building in Barnsley

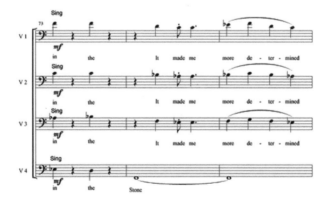

CHAPTER SIX

The Changing Face of Barnsley in the 1930s

Jayne Dowle, Barnsley

Stand on the front steps of University Centre Barnsley today and before you is a panorama of Barnsley's history. Many of the shops and buildings were already here in 1932, when the building was officially opened on 10 October, as Barnsley's Mining and Technical College by Alderman Henry Milnes Walker JP, Chairman of the Higher Education Committee.

However, the nineteen thirties were bringing a colossal scheme of change and regeneration to Barnsley. The building of the College and the Town Hall remain as two of the most outstanding examples of this ambition. The immediate area surrounding these twin pillars of achievement, down Market Hill and into the heart of the town itself, underwent a revolution during this period. It was not only the new buildings, but the changing nature and function of the town centre, and the increasing prosperity and sophistication of the people who lived in Barnsley, which made the decade of the nineteen thirties such a crucial one in the development of the town.

The process of change was driven by four major factors: the growing recognition of education, coupled with the increasing mechanisation of the mining industry, which required a supply of highly-trained workers; the relocation of residents from sub-standard housing in the town centre to new council estates on the periphery, freeing up land for the new College and Town Hall; the drive for civic pride, to establish Barnsley town centre as a major business and administrative centre for the Borough; and overall, it was underpinned by the desire for Barnsley to present a modern front to the world by transforming itself from a extended medieval market town into a trading, social and cultural focus of South Yorkshire.

The subject of education is dealt with in detail elsewhere in this book by Professor Tim Thornton and Martyn Walker, so this chapter will concentrate on the subjects of town centre redevelopment, the evolution of civic pride, and the development of the identity of Barnsley in the nineteen thirties.

In order to appreciate how Barnsley had evolved to this stage, it is important to consider certain aspects of the topography of the borough. From its earliest incarnation, the town centre formed a hub for the outlying satellite villages.

With the coming of large-scale mining when the Barnsley Bed and Silkstone coal seams were exploited in the mid- to late nineteenth century, and the subsequent increase in population, as single men and families flocked into the area for work, this arrangement did not alter, but intensified. The Inspector of Mines Reports show that in 1851 11,750 men were employed in the South Yorkshire coalfield. By 1890, this had risen to an estimated 41,000 and by 1924, it was 122,582.[1] Smaller, virtually self-sufficient townships such as Wombwell, Hoyland and Royston did flourish, but the dominant Barnsley characteristic of surrounding pit communities feeding into the town centre was developed. Although daily needs could usually be serviced within industrialised but still semi-rural villages, such as Dodworth, Darfield and Worsbrough, the concept of 'town' as a place where business was done, where major shopping trips took place and where transport radiated to and from became entrenched.

In 1902 The Barnsley & District Traction Company began a shuttle service from Smithies via Barnsley town centre to Worsbrough Dale and Worsbrough Bridge. This made trips to Barnsley and back a possibility for those who had previously been confined to their villages, unless they were prepared to walk or cycle. Elizabeth Laughton, born in 1903, recalled in

---

1. Alan Hill, *The South Yorkshire Coalfield* (Stroud: Tempus, 2001), p. 17.

an interview in 2005 that when she was pregnant with her son in the nineteen thirties she had to take the tram from Worsbrough Dale to the maternity hospital at Pindar Oaks, on Sheffield Road, in labour, being jostled along with 'the colliers in their pit muck'.[2]

Brian Elliott explains that after the Norman Conquest 'the original Saxon hill-top settlement [of Barnsley] was eventually superseded in favour of a planned new town strategically sited less than a mile to the south where communications were far better. A characteristic street pattern was laid out, centred on a broad market place.'[3] In 1249, the Cluniac monks, based at the priory of St John at Pontefract, under whose control the town came, were granted a charter from Henry III to hold a weekly Wednesday market and an annual four-day fair in October. Elliott notes that 'as early as 1280 the primary settlement was already being referred to as Old Town or Old Barnsley.' The 'new' Barnsley developed with the market at its centre. Its position as a market town was consolidated over the centuries; Barnsley became the central focus for outlying rural villages and farms, especially on market days.

A contributor writes in *The Bus to Barnsley Market*, a compilation of experiences about Barnsley published in 1989: 'There is a big sense of belonging in Barnsley, a lot of civic pride. Barnsley market is part of that, it is a focal point for the community. Not just Barnsley itself though, the community in this whole area is not fragmented like some, so people from the outlying villages see this market as very important and are prepared to trail ten miles to come here. It's a day out as much as anything.'[4]

---

2. Interview with Jayne Dowle, Aug 2005.
3. Brian Elliott, 'Glimpses of Mediaeval Barnsley', in Brian Elliott (ed.), *Aspects of Barnsley*, 7 (Barnsley: Wharncliffe Books, 2002), pp. 26–27.
4. Brian Lewis, Mel Dyke, Ian Clayton, *The Bus to Barnsley Market: Journeys into Experience* (Castleford: Yorkshire Arts Circus, 1989), p. 93.

By the eighteenth century, Barnsley had also become a centre of the linen trade. In 1793 in a survey of Yorkshire it is stated that, 'Barnsley carried on a considerable trade in wire, and had manufactories for bleaching and weaving linen yarns, which is in a flourishing state.'[5] The population of Barnsley in 1750 was 1,740. In 1801, when the first official census was taken, it was 3,606. At this time the report says about 500 handlooms were employed in the town. By the 1851 census, notes Melyvn Jones, there were 'more than 4,000 handlooms located in the town centre in nearly 800 loomshops ... [A]lthough domestic linen loomshops were widely distributed throughout the town, the greatest concentration lay between the bottom end of New Street in the north, Wood Street in the south, Silver Street in the west and Duke Street in the east, that is the area known as the "Barebones", with extensions eastwards along Copper Street and Union Street to Sheffield Road and beyond in Taylor Row, King Street and Rodney Row.'[6] So it was the linen-weavers, rather than the miners, who first seriously consolidated the position of Barnsley as a population centre.

Many historians, including Joseph Wilkinson, in his *History of Worsbrough*, published in 1872, have noted the importance of Barnsley on stage-coach routes between London and the north of England. Wilkinson notes that in 1790 there were two Leeds-London mail coaches a day, plus stage-coaches to London, Nottingham, Sheffield, Birmingham, Leeds and Derby, and innumerable wagons and carriers.[7]

This gives us some indication as to why Barnsley became such a well-known town on the 'national map' and an important

5. Barnsley British Co-operative Society, *The Coronation History of the Barnsley British Co-operative Society Limited, 1892–1902* (Manchester: Co-operative Wholesale Society's Printing Works, 1903), p. 195.

6. Melvyn Jones, 'The Migration History of a Linen Weaving Family, 1798-1932', in Brian Elliott (ed.), *Aspects of Barnsley*, 6 (Barnsley: Wharncliffe Books, 2000), pp. 54–55, 56.

7. Joseph Wilkinson, *History of Worsbrough* (London: Farrington & Co.; Barnsley: T. Lingard, 1872), pp. 162–63.

strategic place on trade, commerce and social routes. The identity of Barnsley is rooted in the town's history as a complicated, complex transport and industrial hub.

By the beginning of the nineteen-thirties, the area which surrounds University Centre Barnsley was undergoing transformation from a narrow Victorian and Edwardian gateway into the town, lined with old shops and tradesmen's yards, into a wide and grand thorough-fare, with the most up-to-date of modern buildings. To the north of the College was an obelisk, which marked the northern approach to the town. Its demolition at the beginning of the decade was symbolic of the clamour for change. The obelisk was close to the top of Old Mill Lane, where the site of Barnsley College is today. It was erected in 1819 and gave its name to a grand house, known as Obelisk House. The Obelisk was demolished in 1931, and the house in 1962. Gerald J. Alliott notes the 'fierce controversy' of 'that relic whilst in the throes of its death pangs'.[8] Between here and the Obelisk was St Mary's Church, still standing today, across St Mary's Gate, next to the College. The noted Barnsley historian E. G. Tasker believed that it was probable that a church had stood on the site since Saxon times.[9] The 'new' Church was consecrated in 1822.

On the site of the new College had been the old Manor House. In a Parliamentary Survey of Barnsley dating from 1649, it was described thus: 'The Manor House ... a capital messuage ... an ancient strong timber house ... consisting of a spacious Hall, two parlours, two other nether rooms with a buttery, 3 lodging chambers [at the south end of the property], kitchen, a parlour, a dairy house with two chambers over them [at the north end].'[10] It is believed that the Manor House was owned by the Duke of Leeds, and became home to a string of worthy Barnsley families, including the Cantors, the Harveys and the Piggotts. By 1928,

8. Gerald J. Alliott, *The Vanishing Relics of Barnsley* (Barnsley: Wharncliffe Publishing, 1996), p. 95.
9. E. G. Tasker, *Barnsley Streets* (4 vols, Barnsley: Wharncliffe Books, 2001), vol. 1, p. 42.
10. Elliott, 'Glimpses of Mediaeval Barnsley', p. 34.

according to a directory, it is described as, 'an unpretentious building at the corner of St Mary's Gate, used for council and committee meetings and as the borough police station.'[11]

When the Manor House was demolished, its functions were dispersed. Many of its administrative elements were transferred to the new Town Hall, which was opened on Thursday, 14 December 1933 by Edward, Prince of Wales.

According to various contemporary records, the Prince was more worried about whether he could do justice to the huge Albert Hirst Barnsley Chop he was served at lunch than about the political controversy which surrounded the cost of the new Town Hall. The menu, devised by Mr and Mrs J L Thornhill of the Royal Hotel, Church Street, featured Barnsley chop, chips – and, bizarrely, tea and toast – followed by peach melba and cheese and biscuits. The Prince said he was 'somewhat alarmed' when faced with the prospect, and sought assurances from the mayor, John Guest, that there would be 'no fine for not finishing it'. This was not the Royal Hotel's first brush with royalty. It was originally called, and has now reverted to the name of, the White Bear. But the old coaching inn had changed its name in 1835, following a visit from Princess Victoria.

The Town Hall, designed by Liverpool architects Briggs and Thornely, had its critics, and even when it was given the go-ahead the planning department was wary of the expense it would incur. It had taken decades to secure agreement from all the interested parties for planning permission for a new building to be granted. In 1914, the local council had obtained the power, in a local Act, to acquire land and build a Town Hall and other buildings, with the cost estimated at around £30,000. Plans were prepared and tenders submitted. But the First World War curtailed the project. It came back onto the agenda in 1923, when the council appointed Messrs Briggs and Thornely as architects. The proliferation of administrative departments, a pressing need for office accommodation, and the extension of the remit of the Borough (Barnsley had

---

11. Brian Elliott, *A Century of Barnsley* (Stroud: Sutton, 2000), p. 51.

become a County Borough on 1 April 1913) drove the desire
to create a purpose-built civic centre for the town. But in 1927,
in the aftermath of the General Strike and in unfavourable
economic conditions, the council decided, owing to the capital
cost involved, to postpone the project indefinitely.

In 1929, however, the Ministry of Labour's Unemployment
Grants Committee took the decision to make grants available
towards construction schemes which would contribute towards
reducing unemployment. A grant for the cost of the new
building, and to the Ministry of Health for sanction to borrow
£130,000 to defray the cost of the scheme, was made. The
Municipal Review for Barnsley, published in September 1931,
records that '[o]fficial sanction to the proposal was subsequently
granted and a beginning was made with the new building last
year.'[12] The *Municipal Review* notes that the need to provide the
town with 'proper civic headquarters' had been clear since
before the First World War. 'In Barnsley the spirit of progress
has always manifested itself in connection with municipal
affairs, but for many years now there has sadly been needed a
central home in which the various activities of the corporation
could be conducted with that facility that makes for efficiency.'

The functions of the new Town Hall were to include the
Council Chamber, a central reception room, five committee
rooms and the Mayor's parlour on the first floor. The
remainder of this floor was to be utilised for the town clerk's
and borough surveyor's departments. The second floor, with
the exception of the water engineer's offices and caretaker's
apartments, was to be devoted entirely to about 8,000 sq ft of
office accommodation, 'thus giving adequate and convenient
accommodation for new departments that may from time to
time be created or for the extension of those already existing,'
the *Municipal Review* notes. In the basement were to be situated
school attendance offices, and storage. There was a further
3,000 sq ft of floor areas that could be utilised as additional
offices or storage in the future.

---

12. *The Municipal Review* (Sept 1931), pp. 347–48.

Critics complained that even though it was providing work for the unemployed, Barnsley people needed new houses more than they needed a new Town Hall, and that the Council was wasting money – £188,000 to be precise – on the project. The most prominent critic of the scheme was George Orwell, who visited the town in 1936 to research his book *The Road to Wigan Pier*. He stayed at 4 Agnes Road, in the house of miner Albert Gray, his wife Minnie and daughters Irene and Doreen.[13] Orwell criticised the council for not providing homes for the town's 70,000 inhabitants, 'not one of whom has a bath in his house!' Gilbert Langstaff, the editor of *The Barnsley Chronicle*, gave *The Road to Wigan Pier* a stiff review on its publication in March 1937, and rejoined the slur on the town with a list of impressive facts and figures: 'actually 9,287 males in Barnsley worked in mines and quarries and all 3,200 council houses had baths, as well as at least some of the 11,298 other working class [sic] houses. And the old Town Hall had been a disgrace, with offices scattered all over town, and the assembly chamber near the police cells.'[14]

On the site of the Town Hall itself had been Lancaster's Yard, which was home to a variety of trades, including Alfred Badger, chemist, Edward Micklethwaite, architect, Charles Fletcher, watchmaker, E Lawson, wireless dealer, Reynolds & Wadsworth, ironmongers, and Mary Ann Eastwood, hairdresser and toy dealer. On the west side of Church Street, behind the College and the Town Hall, was a whole self-contained community of houses, schools and even a fire station. Much of it was substandard early nineteenth century housing, and demolition had commenced in the nineteen twenties. In 1852, the Ranger Report for the Board of Health noted that in Harrison's Yard, adjoining Westgate, there were nine houses and one privy for thirty-two people, on Pinfold Hill, adjoining Shambles Street, there were six houses and one privy for thirty people, and in

13. Rose Johnston, 'George Orwell and the Road to Pogmoor Sands', in Brian Elliott (ed.), *Aspects of Barnsley*, 5 (Barnsley: Wharncliffe Publishing, 1998), p. 138.
14. *Barnsley Chronicle*, cited in Johnston, 'Orwell', p. 145.

Liddall's Yard there were nine houses and one privy for thirty-seven people.[15]

Street names such as School Street, Roper Street and North Pavement have now disappeared for ever, but there are still plenty of people who have living memories of this area. One well-remembered pub was the three-storey Black Boy inn which came down in 1956. The schools included the forerunner of the present St Mary's School, now on Stocks Lane. In 1931, there were 6,956 people living in the Central Ward; by 1961, this had fallen to 3,339, according to census figures. Many of the families who lived here were dispersed to the new council-built housing estates which started to go up after the First World War in response to the government campaign to build 'Homes for Heroes'. Led by Christopher Addison, this was established in 1919, under the provisions of the Liberal government's Housing and Town Planning Act. The target was 500,000 new houses in three years. The original legislation was superseded by the Conservative Prime Minister's Neville Chamberlain's Housing Act in 1923, the Labour government's Wheatley Act in 1924 and by Arthur Greenwood's Housing Act in 1930. This gave local authorities the power to demolish houses which were dangerous to health or unfit for human habitation, and put the obligation on them to re-house the tenants. It paved the way for the large-scale social housing schemes which developed around the periphery of Barnsley town centre in the nineteen-thirties.

In Barnsley, the first of these council estates were built at Cundy Cross, close to the site of the ancient Cluniac Monk Bretton priory, Wilthorpe, Lundwood. Smithies, Ardsley, and Worsbrough Common, which marks the highest spot in the centre of Barnsley.

Such developments were the stimulus for strong emotions, as one recent observer makes clear:

---

15. William Ranger, 'The Privy Accommodation', *Ranger Report* (London: George E. Eyre and William Spottiswood, 1852), pp. 68–69.

When people talk about slum clearance it brings great offence to me. Neither I nor any of my family have been born or lived in a slum. Our houses have been castles. What cannot be denied, though, is that a lot of housing in central Barnsley has been knocked down. For instance, the area where the Town Hall is now situated, was cleared, and residents of the area were evacuated to Lundwood in the nineteen-thirties. If you like, it was an early work programme to ease local unemployment.[16]

These terraced houses behind the Town Hall and College had stood within spitting distance of some of the grandest houses in Barnsley town centre. The 'Huddersfield Road' area was where solicitors, doctors, and better-class shopkeepers lived in full-scale Edwardian splendour. Around Sackville Street, mill-owners such as Robert McLintock and John Henry Qualter built grand family homes so they could be close to work and keep an eye on their workers. Providence Villa, on Prospect Street, was built in 1851 by James McLintock. Many of the families who lived in the terraced houses around here would have worked at one of the numerous mills or factories around the Town End.

Although the Town Hall dominates the approach to Huddersfield at the south end of Church Street, there are plenty of other grand buildings worthy of note from Church Street down Market Hill. Indeed, since much of the original Pitt Street, described by Pevsner as 'the best street in Barnsley',[17] was gradually decimated by demolition between the nineteen thirties and the nineteen eighties, Church Street and Market Hill are now the locations of some of the town centre's most notable architecture.[18]

---

16. Brian Lewis, Ian Sawyer, Lans Stevenson, Colleen Vernon, *Barnsley Seams of Gold* (Barnsley: Open College of the Arts, 2001), p. 37.
17. Nikolaus Pevsner, *The Buildings of England, Yorkshire West Riding* (Harmondsworth: Penguin, 1967), p. 94.
18. Johnston, 'Orwell', p. 145.

On Church Street, directly opposite the College, is the Cooper Gallery. The earliest element of this building dates from 1660, when it was the Thomas Keresforth Grammar School, set up to educate the children of Barnsley for free – if their parents were not worth £200 in land and debtless goods. In 1847, an extension, known as the Church Institute, was added, and it was briefly used as a Conservative Reading Room. Then between 1874 and 1912, before the new Grammar School was built on Shaw Lane, it was Holgate Grammar School, where young men of good families studied. Its famous pupils include Joseph Locke, the railway engineer. When the school moved out, the Worsbrough industrialist and philanthropist Samuel Joshua Cooper purchased the building, and made it available to the National Reserve for headquarters and a club. Before he died, he made a bequest for it to become an art gallery. During the Second World War, the Cooper Gallery, as it was named, was requisitioned as an additional wing to the old Beckett Hospital, which stood on Churchfields. It did not re-open as a gallery until 1951.

On the same side of Church Street, as well as some of Barnsley's oldest-surviving shops, recognisable by the stone roofs and protruding timbers, are some excellent examples of solid old buildings, such as the mellow stone branch of Barclays Bank, where banking started in 1796. Further down from the Cooper Gallery, at the top of Regent Street, is the Barnsley Permanent Building Society. This stunning example of nineteen thirties architecture was built in 1939, on the site of Dr Sadler's house, which had been pulled down in 1924. Dr Sadler was the Medical Officer of Health for the town, and had been active in the fight against cholera in the nineteenth century. Further down now stands the Royal Bank of Scotland. Originally, there was a pub on this site, but from 1828 onwards it became a news-room, a Mechanics' Institute, and a Post Office. In the middle of the nineteenth century part of this stretch of buildings down Market Hill became the 'Commerce or Commercial Buildings', which housed shops and offices, including those of the town clerk, Henry Horsfield. The Corinthian Pillars which decorated the front of the group of buildings were removed in 1879 and purchased by the council for £50, and have stood in Barnsley's Locke Park since.

At the opposite side of Market Hill, however, on the corner of Shambles Street facing the Town Hall, the former home of the Halifax Building Society remains. Now the Blah Bar, a popular bar and restaurant, it was built in 1935, and originally occupied by Edgar's Gowns. Between 1942 and 1956, its impressive façade formed the entrance to York County Savings Bank, but it is probably best remembered as the site of the Halifax Building Society, which had premises here from until recently.

Although Barnsley suffered from unemployment and economic depression in the nineteen twenties, it is clear that as the nineteen thirties dawned, the town began to re-assert itself. A new class, a middle class which was not directly linked to trade or to the mining industry, began to make its presence felt. This can be evidenced by the development of private houses around the town centre, to house the teachers, the office employees and the shop-workers who required family accommodation. Johnston notes that in 1936, new houses had been built at Gawber and were selling for £395 and on the Cockerham Estate off Huddersfield Road, further properties were for sale for between £550 and £800.[18] In 1937, an advertisement carried in the *Barnsley Official Record* for Barnsley Permanent Building Society, promoted 'advances are now being made on Security of House property at 4 and a half per cent' – to borrow £500 cost £2.11.3.[19] Johnston also cites a contemporary advertisement:

Over 90 houses sold out of 100 on our Limes Estate Gawber Road – this speaks for itself – Book One of Few Remaining Sites NOW from £395 – DEPOSITS FROM £20 – £5 BOOKS SITE. Large number already sold on our POGMOOR ROAD ESTATE THIS ESTATE HAS JUST COMMENCED – Call at Limes Estates Office, or write – REAL ESTATES (DON) Ltd. TEL BARNSLEY 261 16, South Parade, Doncaster.

---

19. *Barnsley Official Guide 1937* (Barnsley, 1937, published as part of the Joy Week Magazine), p. 8.

It was clear that Barnsley was changing. A new identity for the town, not tied up with its ancient reputation as a market town, or its coal-mining, or its glass and textile manufacture, was beginning to emerge.

This demanded modern transport. If stage-coach routes had helped to put Barnsley on the map in the eighteenth century, and tram routes had helped to bring in people from outlying villages at the start of the twentieth century, then in the nineteen thirties it was the new bus station which kicked off a transport revolution. It was preceded by the demise of the tramways. In the late nineteen twenties, the Yorkshire Traction Company was still running tramcars, but had added 142 motor-buses to its fleet. Advertisements proudly declared that the company had 164 services to towns and villages in the surrounding area. The trams were being superseded by the steady progress of the bus. Between 1929 and 1930 a Bill went through Parliament to permit the abandonment of the tramways. Stephen Farnsworth and Roger Glister note that 'this was implemented on 1 September 1930 when the Lord Mayor of Barnsley drove the last tram into the depot.'[20] Farnsworth and Glister record that a terminus had first emerged in the town centre for the trams, starting out as a line of 'stands' on Eldon Street. The terminus rapidly expanded, however, and by 1936 the bus operators were using stands all over the town centre, in Kendray Street, Midland Street, Church Street, Doncaster Road, Peel Street and at the Gas Nook. The chaos, especially on market days, can only be imagined.

As the bus services proliferated, it became obvious that a new, purpose-built bus station was urgently required to accommodate the passengers and traffic. In October 1936, a site was identified adjacent to the London & North Eastern Railway's Barnsley Exchange Station and the viaduct of the Court House Station, served by the London Midland and Scottish Railway. The contractors, William Johnson & Son of Park Street, Wombwell, started work on 27 October 1937, and took just over a year to

---

20. Stephen Farnsworth and Roger Glister, *Barnsley Buses* (Barnsley: Wharncliffe Books, 2001), pp. 8–9.

build the brand-new station, an amazing feat considering the size and scale of the facility. Barnsley's new 'Omnibus Station' was opened on 13 December 1938. Immediately, it was recognised as 'one of the best bus stations' in Yorkshire, and within months it was the starting and stopping point 'for up to 3,000 arrivals and departures a day.'[21] 'When the new facility opened in 1938, it was acclaimed as one of the best bus stations in the county, boasting progressive features such as toilets with hot and cold running water, and a catering section considered to be "the best in the business".'[22] The café 'was franchised to Godley's whose café was capable of seating one hundred diners for anything between a sandwich and a hot meal.'[23]

The 'threepenny bit', an area located on the Centre Island, became a crucial rendezvous for young men and women, coming into town from outlying areas to meet friends and potential partners on the 'Bunny Run' around the streets.

As already noticed in passing, when the bus station opened in 1938 there were still two railway stations in the centre of Barnsley, the Exchange (or the 'Bottom station') and the Court House station. There was also another train station at Summer Lane, strategically-placed to handle freight from surrounding industry. It is interesting to note a peculiar feature of town centre transport, the viaduct which brought the railway line above the bus station into Court House station. The viaduct was to be the downfall of Court House station – it became increasingly expensive to maintain. In 1960, a decision was made to close the Court House station and a new junction designed to allow more trains into the Exchange station was built instead. The viaduct was demolished in 1970.

By the nineteen thirties, because of the general economic downturn, and cheaper goods from Scotland and Ireland, the Barnsley linen trade had dwindled to a few specialist firms,

---

21. Farnsworth and Glister, *Barnsley Buses*, p. 99.
22. Phil Holland and Mark Smith, *Memories of Barnsley: Nostalgic Photographs of Local Places, People and Events, 1930 to 1970* (Halifax: True North Books, 1997), p. 13.
23. Farnsworth and Glister, *Barnsley Buses*, p. 99.

including a company which specialised in tea-towels at Gawber. However the association with fabric-making and its related trades characterised the economy of the town – especially for young women workers. It was young women such as this who used Barnsley bus station every day: for work, and for leisure. Thousands of women were employed in sewing factories, such as Empire Mills, on Stocks Lane, which made shirts and formed part of the industry around the Town End area. In the early twentieth century, this had been a hive of industrial activity which included the engineering company Qualters & Smith, countless forges and workshops, a blacksmiths, a sawmill, and even an abattoir.

The school-leaving age was fourteen, until the 1944 Education Act raised it to fifteen. Although the new College was to offer opportunities for further study, it was natural for a young working-class woman in the nineteen thirties to take a job as soon as she left school. Since the First World War, fewer young women had been going into domestic service, which had been a traditional channel for working class girls for centuries. Despite various government schemes to encourage more girls to enter domestic service, the majority began to prefer the higher wages and freedom of working in a factory, a shop or an office. Any money these girls had left after paying 'board' to their parents at home was spent on the latest glamorous things; cosmetics, clothes, hair-styles and shoes, and, as will be seen, there were plenty of shops in Barnsley where they could indulge themselves.

From its earliest days, Barnsley had been renowned as a trading centre, and the market was at the centre of this. As Dyke observes, '[t]hey used to say that if you could not buy it on Barnsley market then they did not make it. They used to bring bus trips from all over the country to see our market.'[24] It is fair to say that in the nineteen thirties, Barnsley Market was enjoying one of its heydays. In the coming decade, the market expanded to occupy four acres over six sites – May Day Green, Lower May Day Green, Market Hill, the New Market, Queen's and Kendray Street. The west side of Kendray Street had

---

24. Conversation with Mel Dyke, May 2008.

originally been a cattle market, but by the nineteen twenties it had become a fish market. Along Midland Street, dating back to the earliest days of the market, was the wholesale fruit and vegetable market, where the warehouses of A Dennis, a long-noted name for fresh produce in Barnsley, operated.

One of the busiest times in the market was late on a Saturday, when the traders would be selling up for the weekend and everything was knocked down in price. A common memory of those who recall the market in the nineteen-thirties is of the mothers, especially those with large families to feed, descending after 5pm to buy up the fish, meat and vegetables cheap.

Dominating though it was, there was more to shopping in Barnsley than its market. There were, for instance, half-forgotten enclaves such as the Gas Nook: a row of ancient shops which stood behind the present market, down towards Pontefract Road. Its name dates back to 1821 and to the gas works which was located there. There was also Sheffield Road. Unlike Huddersfield, Racecommon and Dodworth Roads, which were mainly residential, and Summer Lane, which was dominated by industry, Sheffield Road was the only main road into Barnsley that was a self-contained shopping district in its own right. At the junction of Sheffield and Doncaster Road stood the imposing Ebenezer Chapel, which closed on Easter Sunday, 1975. A contemporary record from the late nineteen-thirties lists a plethora of shops and services on Sheffield Road, including eleven butchers, nine furniture shops, two libraries, two dairies, two corn dealers, one milk bar, and – a real sign of the times – six tobacconists.[25] Doncaster Road also had its fair share of shops, including Charlesworth's Butchers, which has certainly been there since the 1930s and is still trading, and also still standing today – but no longer accepting guests – the Model Lodging House, which catered for the homeless.

In Barnsley town centre itself, there were shops which are still landmarks today, such as Benjamin Harral's 'Ring Shop' whose 1906 grand frontage is still just about discernable under

25. Brian Elliott, *Barnsley's History from the Air* (Barnsley: Wharncliffe Publishing, 1994), p. 71.

layers of white paint. Until recently is was home to Lancaster's estate agents after it ceased trading as a jeweller's in 1988. On Shambles Street, The White House furniture store offered 'a unique system of dignified easy payments'.[26] And, of course, there was the Arcade, which was constructed in 1893, and boasts a gracious Victorian roof and cobbled floor.

The main shopping thoroughfare, however, was – as it still is – Cheapside. From the eighteenth century, this area had been dominated by small workshops, such as nailmakers, shoemakers, felt-makers, breechesmakers and joiners. The nineteen twenties had, however, according to Elliott, already marked a time of 'great commercial change' for Cheapside.[27] Of twenty-two Cheapside shops registered in 1928, only ten could trace their occupancy before 1914. One of these was Baileys, with its famous sign of a stork and its slogan 'We supply all but the baby', which set up in 1883. The shop later moved to New Street, and the sign moved to take up residence at Elsecar Heritage Centre, to the south of Barnsley. Cheapside was where the famous Barnsley butcher Albert Hirst set up his shop in 1923, the man who, as already mentioned, provided the meat for the Prince of Wales' lunch when the Prince came to open the Town Hall. Cheapside was also home to three tailors – Alexandre Ltd, which started trading in 1925, Crowes, which opened in 1928, and Montagu Burton Ltd, which started in the same year and moved into its grand landmark premises – latterly MacDonalds, and now home to the Halifax Building Society – in 1930. This was not to mention the Co-op's outfitting department.

Despite – or perhaps because of – the threat of poverty that was never far from so many Barnsley residents, there was always a determination to look smart, even in straitened circumstances. In the nineteen thirties, three major High Street names arrived in Barnsley: Woolworths opened in 1932, taking over the former site of the Maypole Dairy Company and Jackson's the Hatters; Marks & Spencer opened in 1937; and Littlewoods came to town in 1939.

---

26. *Barnsley Official Guide 1937*, pp. 50–51.
27. Elliott, *Barnsley's History from the Air*, p. 10.

The Barnsley British Co-operative Society also thrived during the nineteen thirties. Its system of giving a bonus, or dividend, to its shareholders was eagerly supported by local people. Many an individual born in the nineteen twenties remembers being taken to the Co-op to be kitted out in new clothes for Whitsuntide. The Co-op was founded in Barnsley in 1862 at a meeting held by nine 'men of vision' at Tinker's Temperance Hotel, May Day Green, led by a Mr George Kay. With £30, they set up the first Co-op shop in Market Street, selling a variety of general goods. In 1885, the Co-op purchased and developed the 'Perseverance Estate' off Summer Lane, which provided a base for many of the Co-op's activities, including baking, butchery, cold storage and the production of mineral water. The Co-op grew to dominate Market Street and Wellington Street, and, as well as food and clothing, its services ranged from a highly popular café at the top of Market Street to funeral services. The Co-op closed its headquarters in Barnsley in the nineteen eighties. The building it had occupied on Wellington Street for more than a century became a public house and a nightclub.

The proliferation of public houses in Barnsley town centre ran in tandem with its development as a market town and position as a major stop on stage-coach routes. On Shambles Street, before the redevelopment of the nineteen-thirties, there were twenty-eight public houses. One of those worth recalling is the Old White Bear, which had its roots even further back than the White Bear across Market Hill where the Prince of Wales dined. Barnsley Library now stands on the site of this public house. It is first mentioned in records in 1717, as a dinner was held here to celebrate Barnsley Races. There are only four pubs actually on Shambles Street now. Only one, the Chocolate Bar (formerly the Three Travellers) is actually in an original public house building.

Although there were plenty of pubs to choose from, many were still not regarded as places where respectable young women might socialise. Exceptions included the Chennells on Wellington Street, which advertised in *The Barnsley Official Guide* in 1937: 'Meet your friends at Chennell's Bars, Wellington Street, Barnsley ... Wines from the Wood, Bass's Ale on Draught, Barnsley's Brightest Bars. Separate Ladies'

Room.'[28] The cinema, however, was a different matter. This was open to all and a place where women could congregate together to see the latest fashions, hear the latest music, and pick up the latest dance-steps from the films. The cinema had the power to expand horizons like no other medium, and its contribution to the growing sophistication of ordinary people should not be under-estimated. It provided them with something to measure their lives against, and something to which they could aspire.

In common with rest of Britain, the nineteen thirties in Barnsley witnessed the coming of a brand-new generation of cinemas. As soon as it opened, in March 1937, The Ritz claimed the reputation of being the grandest cinema in town. It was built on Peel Street, close to a site that had previously been home to the Pavilion cinema and, before that, in 1909, during a brief fad for 'rinking', the Pavilion ice rink. The Ritz was designed by Beverley and Verity, renowned cinema designers who also built the Carlton in Haymarket and the Plaza in Lower Regent Street, London.[29] If the Town Hall and the new College were outstanding examples of civic architecture, the Ritz, with its neon-lit façade and capacity of 2,000, was the pinnacle of popular glitz and glamour. Writing in the *Barnsley Chronicle* in 1980, John Threlkeld described the Ritz as a place where 'luxury and bad taste met and blended'.[30] The foyer was like a cavern and the pay-boxes stood, like sentry-boxes, half way between the doors and the stalls. The slightly curved stairs hugged the walls of the foyer and led to a carpeted area where there were chandeliers and garish mirrors. An advertisement in the *Barnsley Chronicle* prior to the opening was more flattering: 'An atmosphere of warmth and wealth is imparted by the decorative scheme in the foyers, repeated in large scale in the auditorium.' The colour scheme was of graded tones of terracotta, peach and gold. Outside, on the stone front, the name Ritz was picked out

28. *Barnsley Official Guide 1937*, p. 94.
29. Kate Taylor, *Barnsley Cinemas* (Loughborough: Mercia Cinema Society, 2008), p. 32.
30. Taylor, *Barnsley Cinemas*, p. 32, citing John Threlkeld, *Barnsley Chronicle*, 10 October 1980.

in Neon lights.'[31] On the bill at the first performance was *My Man Godfrey*, starring William Powell and Carole Lombard. Special gala seats cost from one shilling. The average wage in Barnsley then was between £2 and £3 a week.

There were many other cinemas in Barnsley, including the Empire, which later became the Gaumont and then the Odeon (and recently re-opened again as the Parkway) on Eldon Street, the Electric Theatre off Church Street, and the Alhambra, the massive cinema at the bottom of Sheffield Road. This had opened to much fanfare as a grand theatre in 1915 – local worthies and lords and ladies attended the opening – but became a cinema in 1927. It ended its days, as did so many other cinemas, as a bingo hall, and was pulled down in the nineteen eighties to make way for its namesake, the Alhambra shopping centre.

Other theatres included the Civic Hall, built in 1867 as the Public and Mechanics' Hall. By the nineteen twenties, it was home to the School of Art, the Library and the Technical School. It was partly the state of over-crowding that this caused which contributed to the need to build new educational facilities such as the Mining and Technical College. Other popular theatres included the Theatre Royal on Wellington Street, which still stands but is now a club, and the Empire Palace, Westgate. Known as the Old Surrey Music Hall, its boards were trodden by famous music hall stars including George Formby and Marie Lloyd. It was demolished in 1954.

What really influenced the evolution of entertainment in the town centre was the growing prosperity of working-class people, and the gradual freedoms allowed to younger women. As the privations of the nineteen twenties gave way to the better conditions of the nineteen thirties, several dance halls opened up in the town centre. Popular venues included the Georges off Pitt Street, and the Baths. This was at Race Street Baths in the winter: the swimming bath was covered over with a sprung-floor. Everyone who remembers it mentions the fact that the

---

31. Taylor, *Barnsley Cinemas*, p. 32.

floor would bounce alarmingly, although of course the water in the bath had been removed from underneath.

From being an uncompromising place of industry, trade and transport, Barnsley emerged from the nineteen thirties as a vibrant and multi-faceted town in which to work, shop, and enjoy oneself. At the top of Market Hill, with the Town Hall and the Mining and Technical College as its pivots, a whole new civic centre had been consolidated. In the heart of the town, the proliferation of shops and places of entertainment, served by a brand-new bus station, helped to transform Barnsley into a social and cultural hub of South Yorkshire.

Yet much of what Barnsley achieved in the nineteen thirties has not been recognised, because the popular perception of the town has been overshadowed by accounts such as those of George Orwell. As Johnston points out, the images which Orwell created, 'like black and white photos taken on a rainy day ... have haunted the town ever since. It is a tribute to the power of his writing that the book has carried an influence beyond its authority. The clichés it produced in the national press, the Barnsley of cobbled streets and back-to-back houses, lasted for decades after the demolition squads had moved in.'[32] It is time to redress the balance, and look beyond the clichés to understand how the Barnsley which was born in the nineteen thirties can provide the inspiration for the Barnsley which will thrive in the twenty-first century.

---

32. Johnston, 'Orwell', p. 147.

CHAPTER SEVEN

'In Search of Phantom Fortunes': Working Class Gambling in Britain 1906–1960s

Keith Laybourn

his chapter is driven by my own personal interest. I was born in Barnsley in 1946 and raised in the nearby village of Monk Bretton. My father was a miner who worked at Monk Bretton pit. It was this pit which kept the village together until it was closed down by Roy Mason, who was Barnsley's MP, and the Labour government, in the late nineteen sixties. As a youngster in the late nineteen fifties I often took small bets for my father and mother to the local bookie on Saturdays, and occasionally ran for him when I was only twelve years of age. I was barely aware that ready money gambling on horses was illegal but then it seemed to me that small scale gambling was an accepted and essential part of the leisure of the working-class culture of mining of which I was a part. I recall winning a £1 on my first bet, of 2s 6d I believe, when *Mr What* won the Grand National in 1958. Gambling seemed to me a natural part of the fabric of working-class life at that time and it was with some regret that I lost an income when the 1960 Betting and Gaming Act was passed and legalised the institutionalisation of off-course ready money gambling on horses through licensed betting shops in May 1961. Until I was fourteen or fifteen, then, gambling was part of my upbringing. Running beat doing a paper round which, thank goodness, I never had to do. It even beat going round the wooden seating at Monk Bretton cricket club looking for change that had fallen out of the pockets of merry and often inebriated spectators on a Saturday and Sunday – although that could be profitable for I once gathered ten shillings from under the seats one early evening. I should explain that the cricket ground at Monk

Bretton was at a steeply sloped angle which allowed batsmen to readily score fours down hill but made them struggle to score even one up the slope. Betting had been a boon to my finances until the licensing of betting shops in 1961 which saw an initial rush of small betting shops give way to the large commercial companies of Hills, Corals, Ladbrokes and Mecca. Even Jordans of Barnsley sold their five shops, the first of which had opened on Huddersfield Road near the centre of town in 1959. Since then I have often wondered about working-class gambling and it has already led me to write a book and an article on the topic.

Gambling is an endemic feature of British society in the twenty-first century with the National Lottery legitimising it from 1994 onwards as an acceptable way of raising money for both the community and sporting projects. It was not always so for in the nineteenth and early twentieth centuries determined efforts were made by the National Anti-Gambling League (NAGL), and associated religious bodies, to control gambling, and particularly working-class gambling. The overtly class legislation that was introduced, and most emphatically the Street Betting Act of 1906 which made illegal off-course ready-money betting in public places, was largely ignored by the working classes who resisted the limited and telegraphed gestures by reluctant police forces and an enlightened Home Office to enforce the legislative impositions of Parliament with which they generally disagreed. Indeed, most detailed social investigations into gambling suggest that a majority of working-class families participated in both illegal of-course ready-money gambling as well as substantial legal on-course gambling, mainly at greyhound tracks.[1] The working classes liked a bit of a 'flutter', particularly on the horses, even if much of it was strictly illegal.

---

1. Central Public Opinion Poll, 1945; *Daily Express* Research, 1948, *News Chronicle* 1948 evidenced in the *Report* of the Royal Commission on Betting, Lotteries and Gaming (1949–51), Chairman H. Willink, London, HMSO, 1951, Cmnd 8190; also quoted in Keith Laybourn, *Working-Class Gambling in Britain c. 1906-1960s: The Stages of the Political Debate* (Lewiston N.Y.: Edwin Mellen Press, 2007), p. 272.

At first, the leading anti-gambling organisation was the National Anti-Gambling League, formed and financed by B Seebohm Rowntree, a Quaker chocolate manufacturer from York and social investigator, from 1890 until it expired in the late 1940s. Yet its activities were supplemented by the Society of Friends at first and, from the nineteen twenties, by the Churches' Committee on Gambling, the Christian Social Council on Gambling and many temporary organisations such as the Christian Emergency Committee that was set up in 1927 to oppose dog racing. Driven on by Rowntree, the NAGL emphasised that gambling should be opposed because it encouraged the poor to waste their money, thus causing poverty, because it was considered to be a corrupting influence on women and children, and since it encouraged a culture of getting something for nothing. Thus, unlike many Christian critics, Rowntree was prepared to accept that gambling was a product of social environment and not necessarily a personal failing. His amended views on gambling appeared in *Poverty and Progress*, his second survey of York conducted in 1936 and published in 1941. What he believed was that the working class he was studying were 'in search of phantom fortunes' and were wasting their money, although he came to accept that the gambling was small scale and regular.

Many contemporaries attempted to resist the accusations laid against gambling by the NAGL and anti-gambling organisations, as will become evident later. In addition, many historians have challenged the various assumptions and dangers of the excesses of working-class gambling. Carl Chinn, in his book *Better Betting with a Decent Feller: A Social History of Bookmaking,* suggests that working-class gambling began seriously in the early nineteenth century before the rapid growth of the sporting press, and that it was a small-scale regular activity by most working-class families – an affordable part of their family budget.[2] Mark Clapson made much the

---

2. Carl Chinn, *Better Betting with a Decent Feller: A Social History of Bookmaking* (London: Aurum, 2004), pp. xvi, 93–96.

same case in his book *A Bit of a Flutter* in which he saw gambling as 'a moderate, economistic and expressive form of recreation', a type of self-help, which the authorities were finally forced to accept.[3] Nevertheless, gambling and gamblers have had a bad press for most of the twentieth century. Indeed, Graham Sharpe, the Media Relations Director of William Hill, wrote, in August 2004, in a 'Foreword' to Carl Chinn's book, that having moved from being a journalist to working for a bookmaker his mother said to him 'From disreputable hack to unscrupulous bookie. All you need to do now is become an estate agent and you've completed the unholy trinity.'[4]

The introduction of the Street Betting Act of 1906 and the conflicts between anti-gambling and pro-gambling forces have led to three questions which will be examined here. First, was gambling an affordable part of working-class leisure or an impoverishing waste? Secondly, why was the Street Betting Act of 1906 introduced? Thirdly, why did it take fifty-five years for this blatant piece of class legislation to be by-passed by the Betting and Gaming Act of 1960 – which allowed licensed off-course betting offices to be opened?

This chapter will argue that, by and large, working-class betting was small-scale, that the anti-gambling lobby was briefly effective between 1904 and 1906, and so made street betting illegal, but that it took more than fifty years for it to be removed from the statute book because even though the Home Office and the chief constables realised that it was futile to operate the Act, and to ban off-course ready-money betting, there were many factors which delayed change. In particular the failure of Winston Churchill's betting duty (1926–9) and the growth of the football pools, greyhound racing and the Irish sweepstakes lottery, in 1930, slowed down the pace of toleration. However, in the long run British society changed and attitudes towards gambling did likewise. It was another

---

3. Mark Clapson, *A Bit of a Flutter: Popular Gambling and English Society, c. 1823–1961* (Manchester: Manchester University Press, 1992), p. 21.
4. Chinn, *Better Betting*, p. xi.

thirty years before, from 1 May 1961, the Betting and Gaming Act of 1960 legalised off-course ready-money gambling in licensed premises driven on by the fact that political parties were becoming increasingly dependent upon illegal lotteries, bingo and gaming activities and because society had become more tolerant of gambling in general.

At the beginning of the twentieth century the working classes were involved in a variety of gambling activities. Apart from gaming with cards, and localized gambling activities such as crown green bowling which was particularly popular in Lancashire, they focused very much on pitch and toss and horse racing. Pitch and toss, which continued with some popularity until the nineteen fifties, was popular in Liverpool; at Coldwell, near Nelson, almost every day 'hundreds of youths and men gathered from all parts of the district'.[5] It was also popular in the North East and Yorkshire although it varied slightly from region to region. Normally, however, contestants pitched at a target to establish who was going to act as the banker although that process was later dropped as bookmakers began to act as bankers. The banker would then establish a circle of punters around him and take bets. A thrower would toss two coins high into the air, so that they would twist, the punter hoping to get two tails to land upwards but losing to the banker if they landed with two heads upwards. One head and one tail would lead to the coins being tossed again. Tossing 'rings', or 'schools', were fairly common until the Second World War but persisted in only a few areas, such as Queensbury, between Bradford and Halifax in the West Riding of Yorkshire. According to one ex-bookmaker, Queensbury was 'the daddy of the tossing rings'.[6] It operated in a ring which was seven yards by seven yards and was often run by Jack Harris, 'a hard man'. At other times it seems to have been run by 'Bump' Roe.[7]

---

5. Ibid., p. 90.
6. Chinn Interviews with bookmakers, Heslop Room, University of Birmingham, Tape 4141 and b, interview with Jack Ingham, 6 May 1988.
7. Ibid., Tape 391 a and b, with Mr. Cooper of Yorkshire, 14 April 1988.

The tossing school normally took place near the Bradford Beck at Queensbury, near an abandoned farmyard, and on one occasion, according to a participant, when the police raided only one man, Crutchy Wilks who had only one leg, escaped by crossing the beck on his crutches when police officers decided to avoid getting wet in the pursuit.[8]

Nevertheless, it was off-course ready-money backing on horses which attracted most interest. Chinn suggests that a substantial proportion of the working class bet regularly on the horses in the early and mid-twentieth century. Many took their bets to betting houses, which were illegal under the 1853 Betting Houses Act, or to bookmakers who operated in the streets and alleyways of towns. The Street Betting Act of 1906 attempted to ban the latter activities. It is, however, clear that a significant proportion of the working classes, possibly the majority, still continued to place regular bets with bookmakers in their houses or on the street. The working class have always gambled but the modern boom appears to have begun in the 1870s and 1880s when newspapers began to publish results starting prices and results.

Illegal off-course bookies prospered in the late nineteenth and early twentieth centuries. They often gathered at meeting and betting grounds such as Williamson Square in Liverpool, Farringdon Street in London, the Midden in Leeds, and other venues. Many extended their operations to factories where their runners or agents gathered bets and often used time bags to store them in what was effectively a form of credit betting which thus made the gambling possibly legal. Every type of shop – from corner shop to fish-and-chip shop – was used by some to cover their illegal bookmaking operations.[9]

This growth of bookmaking was underpinned by a culture of gambling which was developing throughout Britain. Newspapers such as *Sporting Life*, *Sporting Star* and the *Sporting Chronicle* began to provide information about horse racing and they themselves began to organise competitions based upon the football pools and other forms of competition. This was

---

8. Idem.
9. Chinn, *Better Betting*, pp. 101–2.

undermined by the Ready Money Pools Act of 1920, only the second real success of the NAGL in the twentieth century, which ended their activities by imposing credit betting instead of ready-money betting on the punters. This meant that the punters could not be forced to pay up a debt which could not be pursued in law.

The working classes also increasingly participated in many gaming activities. Whist and partner whist were very popular but normally regarded as illegal, because they were initially regarded as relying upon chance rather than skill and were thus illegal under the 1823 Lottery Act. The Home Office generally took a lenient attitude towards whist drives and advised the police to ignore them although during the Second World War there was increased police action against card games, which were represented as being unpatriotic. Indeed, the Blackpool Chief Constable became obsessed with the need to stamp out gaming. So persistent was he that in one case a defendant, Mr Bernard, who was a corporal in the RAF, stated that:

We are all fighting for freedom but what kind of freedom is this? I was playing marbles at the age of eight. At 14 I was tossing pennies, a cruel offence. At 17 I went into the Army and started to play pontoon and, worse than that, poker, all offences against the law. Yet a wealthy man can ring up a bookmaker and have a bet on a horse. I hope that we are fighting for the day when we can have a game of cards when we want.[10]

The working class were all too aware of the class distinctions that existed in both gambling and gaming. These distinctions were encouraged by the NAGL which was formed in 1890. It began in York and quickly spread throughout the country but was remarkably unsuccessful in the eighteen nineties. The original impetus for it had come from F A Atkins, editor of *Home Words* and the religious periodical *Young Man* who

---

10. The National Archives of the UK at Kew, HO 45/20540, containing court cases in the *Lancashire Daily Post*, 6 May 1941 and the *Manchester Guardian*, 14 Feb 1942.

responded to the anti-gambling call of Hugh Price Hughes, the 'self-appointed keeper of the Nonconformist Conscience'.[11] Its main purpose was to vehemently oppose every form of betting and gambling. In its early years the League was led by John Hawke, the honorary secretary, and later by J. M. Hogge, who became secretary in 1906. John Gulland, an Edinburgh solicitor and Whitehall civil servant in the nineteen thirties, joined at about this time and eventually replaced Hogge in 1919. The NAGL aimed to oppose 'every form of Betting and Gambling' and to 'diffuse among all classes of the community useful information; and to promote reform by legislation and effective administration of existing laws and bylaws.'[12] These objectives were issued in all the copies of the *Bulletin* which it issued twice per year until it went quarterly in August 1910. The *Bulletin* also published anti-gambling poems such as this one which appeared in 1895:

> He saw a ragged-breek'd urchin run
> A-shrieking out! 'All the winners!!!'
> And the Devil smiled, as he sniggered, 'What fun!
> What a bait for the greed-fired sinners!
> When the gambling demon is awake,
> Half the imps may be idle snoosers
> But wouldn't it sell if I published – from Hell –
> My record of 'All the Losers!
> Of all the primrose paths 'tis the Betting trade
> Leads straightest to perdition,
> And all the losses each day (of their souls) I would say
> Would fill a big 'Speshul Edition!!'[13]

---

11. Evidence of John Gulland, of the NAGL, in the NAGL Statement to the Royal Commission on Lotteries and Betting, *Minutes*, 30 Sept 1932.
12. Taken from J. R. MacDonald, *Ideal Citizenship* (London, 1905) published by the NAGL. MacDonald was a leading figure in the emergent Labour Party and Labour's first prime minister in 1924.
13. NAGL, *Bulletin* vol. 1, no.10, 10 May 1895, p. 103. The rhyme was later published as 'All the Winners' in *Punch*, 12 May 1895, p. 225.

In 1897 John Hawke won a High Court case, *Hawke v. Dunn* which ruled that a betting ring at Newmarket was a public place within the meaning of the 1853 Betting Houses Act. The issuing of starting prices there was thus illegal. This judgement was overturned within four months by the Jockey Club when Charles Powell, a clerk at Kempton racecourse, obtained a share of Kempton Park and then issued a writ against the company for an injunction of restraint in contravention of the 1853 Betting Houses Act which would force the authorities at Kempton to provide betting facilities. The contrived *Powell v. Kempton* case overruled the *Hawke v. Dunn* judgement. The issue was taken to the House of Lords but the *Powell v. Kempton* judgement was upheld. The NAGL was thus unable to stop gambling in the Tattersall's rings on racecourses throughout the country. This forced the NAGL to drop attempts to control all gambling and to focus upon the easier target of working-class gambling. It became convinced that working-class gambling was immoral and should be stopped. B. Seebohm Rowntree recognised that working-class gambling was rife, and studied it in his survey *Poverty and Progress* (1941) but suggested that the working classes would not gamble if they had better housing and living conditions and thus implied that gambling was a product of a particular social environment rather than a personal failing. The NAGL therefore led numerous campaigns to control the 'tipster' press, and produced a large number of pamphlets that revealed the pitfalls of gambling, such as *Betting: A Boy to a Bishop, The Gambling Tree and its Fruit, Shall I Bet?* and *Why not make Money without Working?*[14] From the eighteen ninetees onwards, then, working-class gambling became the focus of the NAGL which claimed that the working classes wasted an enormous amount of money on gambling. The fact is that there is little evidence to suggest that this was the case.

There are, of course, no precise figures for the level of gambling in Britain in the early twentieth century, although one estimate for 1905 suggested that the level of gambling had

---

14. There are no dates to these pamphlets.

reached £50 million, and that there were about 20,000 bookmakers.[15] During the inter-war years there was much speculation that it varied between about £50 million and £500 million, and even occasionally some recognition that these figures were likely to be turnover and not a loss of income by gamblers. The Rev E Benson Perkins, of the Wesleyan Methodist Church's Social Welfare Department, published numerous pamphlets and books during the inter-war years, including *Betting Facts* and *The Peril of the Pools*, and generally estimated that gambling exceeded £50 million per year although the figure was raised over time.[16] The Royal Commission on Lotteries, Betting and Gaming (1932–3) received estimates which varied between about £100 million and £500 million. The NAGL regularly estimated the gambling bill to be about £350 to £400 million in the late 1930s.

Most of these early estimates were little more than wild guesses. However, they became more accurate from the nineteen thirties onwards. Rowntree's *Poverty and Progress* suggested that the working classes of York were spending small amounts of about one shilling per week on the football and one to two shillings on off-course ready-money gambling on horses. 'One inveterate gambler told our investigator that he'd rather "have six penn'orth of hope than six penn'orth of electricity"'.[17] The Social Survey of Betting (1951) suggested that rich men on £10 or more a week usually staked 4s 6d per week whilst much less well-off working men on £3 per week

---

15. *Chiswick Times*, 2 June 1905, 'The Street Betting Evil' quoted in Chinn, *Better Betting*, p. 94.

16. E. Benson Perkins, *The Problem of Gambling* (London: Epworth Press, 1919); *Betting Facts: Being an Account of the Facts on Betting Given in Evidence before the Select Committee of the House of Commons on Betting Duty* (London: Student Christian Movement, 1925); *Gambling and Youth* (London: National Sunday School Union, 1933); *Gambling in English Life* (revised edn, London: Epworth Press, 1950), and others.

17. B. Seebohm Rowntree, *Poverty and Progress: A Second Social Survey of York* (London: Longmans, Green, 1941), p. 403.

merely staked 2s 6d. Many women did the pools with their husbands, by themselves or with group of friends or workers.[18] The Hulton Readership Survey of 1949–50 estimates were slightly higher with men staking 3s 10d and women two shillings. It reported that about one third of women bet on the pools, and that they represented about twenty per cent of the pools market although their average stake was small at about 3s to 4s.[19] This corresponds with the Sherman survey submitted to the Royal Commission on Betting, Lotteries and Gaming (1949–51) which indicated that out of 250,000 coupons submitted each week 65 per cent of the coupons were for less than 3s and eighty-five per cent for less than 10s. The average for each individual, rather than each coupon, was estimated to be even less at 2s 6d during the 1949–50 season.[20]

From the later, more detailed surveys, it is thus clear that gambling was ubiquitous amongst the working classes. By the late twentieth century more than half of them gambled regularly on the football pools. Although there is no absolutely precise evidence on the extent of illegal off-course ready-money gambling on the horses, evidence suggests that it was endemic amongst the working classes. Where there is evidence of the amount gambled it is clear that the working classes gambled less than their middle-class counterparts, though this sum represented a higher proportion of their income from which they expected and got returns. In the end, the evidence supports the views of Clapson and Chinn that small regular amounts, rather than large pauperising sums, were spent on gambling by the majority of working-class families. This was a finding that did not go down well with the NAGL which persistently attempted to control working-class gambling through legislation even though it is clear that its major success, the 1906 Street Betting Act, was unenforceable and a waste of police time.

---

18. Clapson, *Bit of a Flutter*, p. 174.
19. The National Archives of the UK at Kew, Ho 333/32.
20. Royal Commission on Betting, Lotteries and Gaming (1949–51) *Final Report* (London, 1951), pp. 36–7.

The Street Betting Act of 21 December 1906 amounted to little more than a page of text but it influenced, and occasionally dominated the way in which the police and the off-course bookmakers operated for more than half a century. It stressed that ready money gambling in public places was illegal and listed the penalties to those who were caught. It was the one great triumph of the NAGL but it took them five years to get the Bill passed. John Hawke, of the NAGL, had first declared to the Select Committee of the House of Lords on Betting that he did not wish to meddle with personal liberty but still desired that bookmakers should 'be placed in the dock'.[21] As a result Lord Davey presented a bill to the House of Lords in 1904. It was delayed and Hawke, oblivious of working-class protests, wrote to A J Balfour, the Prime Minister, in May 1905 stating that 'May I implore you to help the Street Bill. There can be no opposition of any importance. Churchmen and Nonconformists are agreed. The Opposition will assent.'[22] It took more than eighteen months for the Bill to be passed through the Lords and the Commons. Whilst strongly supported, one of its parliamentary opponents, C Hay, observed that the Bill made 'one law for the rich and another for the poor'.[23]

The 1906 Act attempted to stop the proliferation of gambling on the street that had occurred because of the 1853 Betting Houses Act which itself was aimed at the ready money betting houses of the working classes and not at the betting clubs of the middle classes. Both acts operated against working-class gamblers and those bookmakers who offered betting opportunities for the streets, in houses, in shops and factories. However, both acts were ineffective in stopping gambling amongst the working classes and it is clear that police action varied immensely; it was intense in Manchester, routinized in

---

21. Select Committee of the House of Lords (1901-2), *Minutes*, q. 230, p. 373.
22. The National Archives of the U.K. at Kew, HO/10301/117059.
23. *Parliamentary Debates*, Commons, 1906, vol. 162, col. 862.

Salford, and barely evident in Leeds.[24] Yet, whether the police took an active or passive approach, they were unable to stamp out off-course ready money betting. The Labour Party, which had supported the 1906 Bill, also began to express its concern at the class bias of the legislation in the nineteen thirties.

The debates surrounding the Betting and Lotteries Bill Act of 1934, which incorporated the recommendations of the Royal Commission on Lotteries and Betting (1932–3), including the decision to retain the ban on public lotteries, were primarily about controlling legal gambling on greyhound racing. Nevertheless, they provoked much wide-ranging comment about the class nature of existing gambling legislation. A typical view was that of J Jones, Labour MP for West Ham Silverstone, who stated that:

The evils of gambling are only discovered when working men start gambling, then it becomes a moral offence. I can go to Throgmorton Street to-morrow morning and see a responsible kind of gambling: nobody calls it street betting. In some streets in my division I can see detectives busily picking up an odd man here or there who is taking betting slips. The other people can gamble with impunity. Those who put a shilling on a horse are heading for Dartmoor but those who put thousands of pounds down are not gambling at all; they are acting in a businesslike way. The Bill does not go so far as I should like it to go. If gambling is wrong, why not deal with it properly on a wholesale scale, and let gamblers go where they ought to go. There ought not to be one law for the rich and another for the poor which is the case today.[25]

---

24. Betting Log Book, covering the Salford areas and particularly the 'South Division', Greater Manchester Police Museum, Newton Police Station, Newton Street, Manchester. See Andrew Davies, *Leisure, Gender and Poverty: Working-Class Culture in Salford and Manchester, 1900–39* (Buckingham: Open University Press, 1992), p. 145.

25. *Parliamentary Debates*, Commons, 1934, vol. 291, 18 June–6 July, cols. 1192-3.

Nevertheless, it should be remembered that the Labour Party, and many of its leading figures such as James Ramsay MacDonald, Labour's first prime minister, were fundamentally opposed to gambling. Much of Labour's opposition was, however, swept away in the general election defeat of 1931, two months after the collapse of the second Labour government. Indeed, in the discussion surrounding the second reading of the 1934 Bill the less critical views of its working-class representatives emerged when Mr. McGovern, the Independent Labour Party MP for Glasgow Shettlestone, reflected that:

> I remember John Wheatley [Minister of Health and Housing in the 1924 Labour Government], when I was a boy of 16, reprimanding a man who was backing a horse. Wheatley said 'I think you are making a great mistake because the bookies are bound to win.' The man looked at Wheatley and said 'Look here John, you don't know what life is. Some people keep rabbits and some keep pigeons, some indeed keep white mice, but my way of enjoying life is occasionally to have a bob or two on a horse. I do that to get a certain amount of enjoyment. Don't take that away from me.'[26]

It is clear that the NAGL and Church interests reached a crescendo of support in 1905 and 1906 which they were never to achieve again. They did not get bills passed on stopping advertisements on gambling before the Great War. They failed to make gambling on greyhound racing illegal on several occasions in the late nineteen twenties and the early nineteen thirties. They failed to get private lotteries banned in 1934, could not stop the football pools when they tried to do so in 1936 and failed to stop the Betting and Gaming Act of 1960 being passed into law with its creation of licensed betting offices. They had some success but their policy of outright banning of gambling almost inevitably failed. There were occasional victories, perhaps the most successful being the

---

26. Ibid., col. 1214, part of the second reading of the Betting and Lotteries Bill, 1934.

passing of the Ready Money Pools Act in 1920. This act only allowed newspapers to offer credit betting on their pools schemes and effectively killed off this form of gambling although the pools companies were able to get round it in the late nineteen twenties by offering credit betting and ensuring that their customers paid up the following week with their next coupon by organising a body to collect the names of defaulters who would be denied betting rights.

The difficulty of the anti-gambling forces is that they were small even though they carried influence in Parliament, divided by religion, and prone to disagreements on the issue of gambling. Within the Society of Friends there was indeed some disquiet at the fact that the Rowntree and the Cadbury families bought a number of newspapers to strengthen the Nonconformist press. Two of these, the *Northern Echo* and *The Star*, were sporting, tipster and gambling papers. From 1907 onwards both papers dropped their adverts for credit bookmakers and refused to publish racing results and *The Star* got rid of 'Captain Coe', its famous tipster. By 1909, however, the sales of these papers were falling. The *Northern Echo's* sales of 30,000 in 1906 (they had been at 5,000 before the Rowntrees took it over) fell to 25,000 in 1909 after which the racing pages and reports were restored to recapture lost sales. B Seebohm Rowntree also arranged with Ernest Parke, the editor of *The Star*, to offer up to four daily editions of the paper while reducing the racing and tipster content in each successive edition. Parke argued that 'a reduction in the amount of racing information would lead to the curtailment of its circulation and the disappearance of profits' and that this should not occur.[27] With Rowntree's permission he restored the 'Captain Coe's Chat' feature. Paul Gliddon's recent article suggests that it was not hypocritical for the major anti-gambler to take the decision

27. TS, letter from Ernest Parke to B. S. Rowntree, 2 March 1911, originally in the Joseph Rowntree Foundation Library but now transferred to the Borthwick Institute, Library of the University of York.

to restore the tipster press to his papers for financial reasons.[28] This as not a view taken by some contemporary writers. Sir Edward Fry in his pamphlet *Betting Newspapers and Quakerism: A Letter Addressed to Members of the Society of Friends*, published in August 1911, complained that 'The National Anti-Gambling League is largely supplied by members of the Rowntree and Cadbury families; those very men are themselves among the principal owners of the Sporting Press.'[29] The Unionist paper *The National Review* suggested that 'Captain Coe' should be renamed 'Captain Cocoa', after the profession of the distinguished owners of the paper.[30]

The legitimacy of the anti-gambling position was further undermined by many chief constables and the Home Office who were doubtful of the dangers of working-class gambling. Robert Peacock, Chief Constable of Manchester, was strongly in favour of the 1906 Street Betting Act Act. In fact he wanted much stricter legislation to allow him to raid the bookmakers but was worried about the lack of working-class co-operation.[31] He sedulously applied the Act in Manchester until his death in 1926. However, most chief constables and the Home Office were critical of it over the next fifty-four years – although much of their criticism was equally aimed at the Betting Houses Act of 1853. The official line was that the police regularly prosecuted the ready money bookies with vigour but there might be a few rotten apples in the forces who accepted bribes and turned a blind eye or pre-warned bookies of raids. The evidence is, however, that police regularly prosecuted bookmakers and often warned them of impending raids.

---

28. Paul Gliddon, 'Politics for Better or Worse: Political Nonconformity, the Gambling Dilemma and the North of England Newspaper Company, 1903–1914', *History*, 87 (2002), pp. 227–44.
29. Anne Vernon, *A Quaker Business Man: The Life of Joseph Rowntree, 1836–1925* (London: George Allen & Unwin, 1958), p. 173.
30. Parke letter to Rowntree, 2 Mar 1911.
31. Select Committee of the House of Lords, 1901-2, *Minutes*, qq. 152–3, p. 9.

Yet it was quite clear that in many areas the police and the bookmakers were operating a relationship, often based upon a mutual understanding rather than corruption, which saw the police effectively charging a rent for gambling in a public place. In Salford, for instance the police kept a record of fifty-one pitches in the 'South Division', returned in alphabetical order, and attached to a log book which covers the period from 1907 to about 1958. The most detailed accounts are for the nineteen twenties when the log book indicates that every pitch was fined £10 in the courts on either two or three occasions per year following two or three raids.[32] Canon Green of Manchester in fact provoked a debate about this when he spoke at Durham Cathedral on 19 November 1932. He stated that:

> Gambling is a grave source of corruption in the police. I do not say that all the police are corrupt. But some of them undoubtedly bribed. How does the bribery occur? The officer will go the bookmaker and say that 'It is time you were on the carpet. Put a dummy at the end of the street and I will take him.' The bookmaker puts in his dummy, the police fine him, and he is fined £10 or a month in prison. If he likes to have him fined he gets a sovereign for the job. If he goes to goal he gets £10.[33]

The resulting debate, between the Manchester and Salford police and Green, raged in the *Manchester Guardian* over the next two weeks with John Maxwell, Chief Constable of Manchester, demanding, but not getting, evidence from Green.

Mr. Jordan, who ran an illegal betting shop on Huddersfield Road in Barnsley in 1959, has stated that 'he had no problem with the police' and recalls how on one occasion he was given prior warning and raided only to have the same officers come

---

32. Betting Log Book, covering the Southern Division of Salford, Greater Manchester Police Museum, Newton Street, Manchester.
33. *Manchester Guardian*, 24 Nov 1932.

in the following week to place a bet.[34] He noted that in the working-class community of Barnsley 'everyone had a bet'. Ken Overton, a Birmingham bookmaker, vaguely referred to the Leeds situation where 'the whole of the police from the chief constable down was conniving at the people breaking the law' and the Chief Constable was sacked.[35] The control of off-course ready money betting was clearly not working.

The Select Committee on Betting Duty, chaired by Sir Henry Cautley in 1923, was one of the first opportunities for the senior police officers to complain that the 1906 Act was unenforceable and placed strain upon the relations between the police and the public. The Chief Constable of Liverpool stated that legalisation would make little difference for 'It is easy now; if you want to bet you can do it.'[36] Cautley subsequently emphasized that the police officers told the same story: 'that betting was the only crime ... in which the sympathy of the public was always with the offenders and the hostility of the public invariably against the police'.[37] The Home Office was concerned about this in its annual meetings with the chief police constables and in the nineteen forties surveyed their opinions on the 1906 Act. The vast majority were in favour of the 1906 Act being withdrawn and the Chief Constable of Leicester added that 'I am unable to find any evidence to show that it is in any considerable degree the cause of crime and lawlessness.'[38] In 1950 Sir Harold Scott, Commissioner of Police of the Metropolis, presented a twelve-page report to the Royal Commission on Betting, Lotteries and Gaming (1949–51) in which he stated that the Street Betting Act was 'class legislation because persons in a good status of life can bet on credit without breaking the law', and that its

---

34. Chinn Interviews, Tape 296 a and b, interview between Carl Chinn and Mr Jordan, 29 Mar 1988.
35. Interviews, Tapes 366 and 367, interview with Ken Overton.
36. Select Committee on Betting Duty, 1923, *Report*, p. 66 q. 1346 (Bigham); p. 58 q.1179 (Caldwell).
37. *Parliamentary Debates*, Commons, 10 June 1926, col. 1747.
38. The National Archives of the UK at Kew, HO 320/12.

enforcement 'does nothing to improve relations between the Police and the public'.[39] He added that the 1906 and 1853 acts were a waste of time for 'in the K Division [of the Metropolitan area] where illegal betting was rife there were 577 arrests in 1948' for which an 'estimated'16,000 man hours had been expended to imprison one person.[40] He added that 'Since experience has shown the impossibility of suppressing cash betting of course it would be better to legalise it under strict control.'[41]

The overwhelming body of evidence suggests that the police felt that the implementation of the 1906 Act, and related legislation, was a waste of time and money to control something which was essentially immoral but not normally criminal. This was an attitude which was also evident in the Home Office. The Cautley Commission of 1923 had revealed the failure of the 1906 Act and had encouraged it to consider the possibility of a Betting Duty, an unsuccessful version of which operated between 1926 and 1929. The Home Office was also interested in the relaxation of the implementation of the rules on gaming and lotteries. Many card games, such as whist, were considered to be lotteries and subject to the 1823 Lotteries Act ban if they were played for money and unless there was an element of skill rather than chance in the game. In a series of memorandums from 1913 to the nineteen thirties, the Home Office emphasised to the police that if whist, and other card games, were small scale then no action should be taken against them.[42] Indeed, the 1921 Memorandum of E. Shortt, Home Secretary, advised that it 'would not be politic to interfere with whist drives of an innocuous nature'.[43] When

---

39. Ibid., HO 335/34, p. 3, evidence presented to the Royal Commission on Betting, Lotteries and Gaming (1949–51).
40. Ibid., p. 5.
41. Ibid., p. 7.
42. The National Archives of the UK at Kew, HO 45/14616, file on 'The Legality of Whist Drives, 24 August 1928'; HO 45/14238, circular sheet on Lotteries (Sweepstakes and Draws) and Whist Drives, circulated Feb or Mar 1930.
43. Ibid., HO 45/14616, file on 'The Legality of Whist Drives'.

the Royal Commission on Lotteries and Betting (the Rowlatt Commission) reported in 1932/33 and wanted the totalisator at greyhound tracks made illegal – which would have made an aspect of on-course ready-money gambling illegal at greyhound tracks but not at the more middle-class attended horse tracks – the Home Office ensured that that did not become part of the 1934 Betting and Lotteries Act.[44]

The fact is that the Home Office, just as much as the police was anxious to get rid of unnecessary legislation in gambling and gaming which might be seen as socially divisive. Indeed, it was J R Clynes, Home Secretary of the Labour Government of 1929 to 1931, who summarised this position in 1930 stating that 'I am glad to have had an opportunity of making this statement, which ought to dispose once and for all the suggestion that there is "one rule for the rich and one for the poor"'.[45] The Chief Constable of Manchester informed Clynes on 28 March 1930 that his aim was 'to promote reasonable uniformity in the enforcement of the law and the avoidance of anything which might suggest partiality or discrimination'.[46]

If both the police and the Home Office were intent on removing some of the legislation on working-class gambling, such as the 1906 Street Betting Act, during the nineteen twenties and the beginning of the 1930s why did this not occur until the nineteen sixties? The 1853 Betting Houses Act and the Street Betting Act of 1906 were practically unenforceable since

---

44. The National Archives of the UK at Kew, Cabinet Conclusions, CAB 23, Cabinet 1 (34) 16 Jan 1934, item 5; Cabinet 8 (34), 7 Mar 1934, Cabinet 11(34), 21 Mar 1934; and Cabinet 17 (34), 25 Apr 1934. Totalisator: the system whereby all bets placed were put into a fund out of which payments would be made.

45. The National Archives of the UK at Kew, HO 45/14238, letter from J.R. Clynes to Sir William Jowett, Attorney General, no date but in Feb or Mar 1930.

46. Keith Laybourn, '"There Ought not to be One Law for the Rich and Another for the Poor which is the Case To-day": The Labour Party, Lotteries, Gaming, Gambling and Bingo, c. 1900–1960s', *History*, 93 (2008), 201–23.

a majority of the nation ignored them. Gaming and lotteries were a minefield which the Home Office was prepared to ignore as long as criminal groups did not become involved. Everything seemed to be set up for immediate and fundamental changes but nothing happened.

It is not easy to establish why there was a delay for another thirty years but it would appear that the Home Office and the police had to give way to the fears of Parliament. The fact is that in the late nineteen twenties and early nineteen thirties the more liberal attitude to gambling was possibly set back by three factors: the equivocation of the Parliamentary Labour Party (PLP), the failure of the Betting Duty of 1926 to 1929, and the new developments in gambling.

The first of these factors, the PLP, has been the subject of a recent article which argues that it was unequivocally opposed to gambling until the 1931 general election swept away much of the old PLP, which fell from 291 to fifty-two MPs; thereafter there was more equivocation as the new body of Labour MPs often opposed gambling but objected to the class discrimination in gambling. This has already been touched upon earlier in this chapter. However, the central point to stress here is that whilst Labour MPs took a more relaxed attitude towards gambling and gaming some retained the lifelong hostility to gambling. Clem Attlee, later a Labour Prime Minister, Aneurin Bevan, the Minister of Health responsible for introducing the National Health Service, George Lansbury, Labour Leader from 1931 to 1935, and others voted against a private member's Lottery Bill in 1932 which was designed to raise money for British hospitals; Bevan and George Thomas, a later Speaker of the House of Commons and a life-long Methodist, opposed the 1934 Betting and Lotteries Bill. Most of the Labour MPs mentioned, and others, were to be found voting against gambling, and the Labour Party today can show remarkable mood changes, as they have done recently in 2006 and 2007 on the issue of the 'supercasino'. If Labour could no longer be relied upon to oppose gambling then they could also not be relied upon to support it. There were also other factors at play.

Winston Churchill had introduced a Betting Duty on gambling in 1926, aimed mainly to raise money from the legal on-, and off-, course credit bookmakers. Churchill's duty was to be based upon a 5 per cent duty on stakes and was to be supplemented by a £10 certificate to be paid by bookmakers in order to raise £6 million. In the end the duty was raised at 2 per cent for on-course and 3.5 per cent for off-course credit bookies. By 1928 the figures were down to 1 per cent and 2 per cent, respectively. And the duty was removed altogether in April 1929.[47] The fact is that bookmakers simply did not pay the duty; James Maclean, a large off-course credit bookmaker in Scotland, paid £48,000 duty in 1927 and claimed that it put him at a disadvantage with the many credit bookmakers who did not pay.[48] As a result the duty raised only £2,700,000 in its best year, 1928. Customs and Excise were reluctant to become involved in such a scheme again and the Home Office developed doubts about licensing off-course bookmakers.[49]

As if an equivocal Labour Party and a failed betting duty were not sufficient a check there was also the problem of the rapid rise of new gambling opportunities – the Irish Hospital Sweepstake Lottery, the growth of the football pools and, perhaps most damaging of all, the runaway success of greyhound racing. All three helped to determine the voting of MPs, many of whom were more positive about gambling than their predecessors.

The Irish Sweepstake Lottery was begun in November 1930 by Richard Duggan, a Dublin bookmaker, and by March 1932 there had been four sweepstake draws that had raised £13,800,000 – of which £2,800,000 went to the twenty-three Irish hospitals involved in the lottery.[50] The first sweepstake was a flamboyant and attractive proposition for the British punter. It was drawn in the Plaza Cinema, Dublin Irish nurses turned the barrel as a blind boy pulled out the numbers under the

---

47. Laybourn, *Working-Class Gambling in Britain*, pp. 127–8.
48. *The Daily Mail*, 29 June 1928.
49. Laybourn, *Working-Class Gambling in Britain*, p. 78.
50. The National Archives of the UK at Kew, HO 45/24919, a Memorandum to the Home Secretary 20 Feb 1932, and a similar memorandum dated 22 Mar 1931.

scrutiny of General O'Duffy, the Commissioner of Police.[51] The tickets were ten shillings each and were based upon the result of the Manchester November Handicap. It was an instant success and there were normally up to three draws per year afterwards based upon the Derby, the Grand National, and other classic races.

The concern of the British government was that a considerable number of tickets, possibly up to £3 million worth, per draw, were purchased by British punters.[52] Indeed, the Post Office had opened up 9,000 letters headed to Dublin to try to stop the illegal movement of tickets.[53] Any suggestion that public lotteries would be legalised in Britain was quickly rejected because of the state fear that it 'would be followed by an immense increase in gambling among all classes'.[54] In the end, the situation did not get any worse, perhaps because of the development of other gambling activities.

The growth of the football pools seemed more threatening to the government. Although the football pools had emerged in Lancashire before the Great War, and been developed in various forms in the newspapers, their great growth occurred during the inter-war years. H Littlewoods was formed by H Littlewoods and John Moores in 1922. From then onwards they mushroomed and although official figures omit the fixed odds given by bookies, it is estimated that by 1938–9 at least £22,500,000 was being spent per year by about a regular six and a half million punters. This figure fell to about £3,500,000 in 1941–2, during the Second World War, but recovered to reach around £66,000,000 per year in 1947–8.[55] It would appear that about half the adult population bet on the pools at some stage in the football season and B. Seebohm Rowntree

---

51. *The Times*, 17 Nov 1930.
52. The National Archives of the UK at Kew, HO 45/24919.
53. Ibid.
54. Ibid., memorandum 24 Feb 1932.
55. Royal Commission on Betting, Lotteries and Gaming (1949–51), *Final Report*, Appendix II, p. 147; Laybourn, *Working-Class Gambling in Britain*, p. 164.

reflected that half the 25,000 or so families in York were betting on the pools and that postal order demand, mainly for 6d. postal orders, rose from 5,300 in a normal week to 17,828 per week in the football season.[56] There were, indeed, up to a hundred companies to bet with in the nineteen twenties although the number gradually slimmed down. Apart from Littlewoods the firms included Vernons, Shermans, Zetters, Copes, Socopools, W S Strange (Edinburgh), T Strange (Edinburgh), Western Pools (Newport), and Gamaco Football Pools (Leeds).

What worried the authorities and Parliament in the inter-war years is that the pools companies got round the Ready Money Football Pool Act of 1920 – which was designed to stop the growth of a variety of pools competitions in newspapers by insisting that they should be based upon credit betting – by setting up an organisation which would check upon defaulters and deny credit and payment to them. It should be remembered that gambling debts could not be recovered in the courts under the 1845 Betting Act. In addition, there was strong pressure placed upon MPs by the football authorities who were strongly opposed to their football fixtures being used for the pools. Sir Charles Clegg, a Nonconformist and Chairman of the Football Association in the nineteen twenties, stated that 'if betting gets hold of football, the game is done for'.[57] The real fear was that gambling would lead to corruption with players becoming connected with pools companies, as occasionally occurred.[58]

The peak of the reaction against the pools occurred in 1935 and 1936 when Charles H Sutcliffe, a Methodist who became the new president of the Football League, pressed the FA Council to ban the advertising of pools coupons in the football programme at a meeting on 7 October 1935. He also persuaded the FA to withhold the publication of football

56. Rowntree, *Poverty and Progress*, p. 403.
57. Perkins, *Gambling in English Life*, cited in Clapson, *Bit of a Flutter*, p. 168.
58. Laybourn, *Working-Class Gambling in Britain*, pp. 157–8.

fixtures until the Thursday or Friday before the fixtures were to be played, although the restriction only lasted for two weeks in February and March 1936. The Football League also claimed copyright over fixtures in the 'Pools War'. The issue continued for a number of years and was not finally settled until 1958 when Littlewoods eventually paid a substantial sum of money to the League.[59]

The public and parliamentary concerns about the football pools were substantial but not as great as those connected with greyhound racing. After a failed attempt to introduce it in the 1870s the first successful greyhound track was opened in Britain at Belle Vue, Manchester, on 24 July 1926. There were 1,700 people at the first meeting but by the spring of 1927 Belle Vue was attracting crowds of up to 25,000. By the end of 1927 there were forty tracks in operation and about 120 companies about to open. By early 1931 there were about 170–175 tracks, another fifty-five organisations held licences to open tracks, and there were about eighteen million attendances at the official tracks. By 1936 about nineteen million attendances were recorded at the National Greyhound Racing Club tracks, although there may have been up to thirty-eight million attendances if all the tracks were to be included.[60] The rate of development was staggering and worrying for the authorities and anti-gamblers.

There was an immediate reaction against greyhound racing from the NAGL, the Evangelical Free Churches and other anti-gambling groups. They feared that the working classes would be increasingly encouraged to gamble and fall into poverty. On the 27 October the Manchester Watch Committee called upon the Home Secretary to introduce legislation to abolish greyhound racing, complaining of 'carelessness' and contempt for 'morality' amongst the young of Manchester.[61] On 13 December 1927 Winston Churchill, the Chancellor of the

---

59. Ibid., p. 158.
60. Ibid., pp. 189–90; Royal Commission on Betting, Lotteries and Gaming (1949–51), *Final Report*, 1951, p. 103 and Appendix II.
61. *Daily Mail*, 28 Oct 1927.

Exchequer, wrote a letter to the Home Secretary, warning him of the spectacle of the 'animated roulette boards' brought about by the development of greyhound racing.[62] In 1928 the Home Secretary informed the Cabinet that 'The principal objection against dog racing is that it is a mushroom growth which threatens to add enormously to betting facilities and, in particular, for betting by many whose means would not permit of their attending horse races.'[63] At the same time John Buchan MP, the famous novelist, enlisted the support of 100 Labour, fifty Conservative and thirty Liberal MPs to press for the Dog Racing (Local) Bill designed to give local authorities the right to license or not to license local greyhound tracks. In supporting the second reading of the Bill on 11 May 1928 he condemned the 'illuminated ribbon of turf' that was threatening to substantially increase working-class gambling.[64] In mid-July 1928, however, the Bill was withdrawn, having been lost in the labyrinth of the Committee stage.

Despite this setback for the NAGL and the anti-gambling fraternity there was still strong opposition to greyhound racing. The development of the Tote, or totalisator on greyhound tracks was seen as worrying by the authorities, even more so when in 1933 it appeared that the use of the totalisators was illegal on greyhound tracks, although it was soon made legal by the Betting and Lotteries Act of 1934. There was, indeed, great concern in the government at the potential that greyhound racing might increase working-class gambling and cause poverty. Indeed, in introducing the 1934 Betting and Lotteries Bill, Sir John Gilmour, the Home Secretary, ignored some of the advice of the Royal Commission on Lotteries and Betting (1932–3) and declared that the Government 'is entirely concerned with the effect of gambling on the social life of the country'. He added that 'My main proposals of the Bill did not interfere with private gambling, but only interfere with social problems as may be regarded as of serious moment to the

---

62. The National Archives of the UK at Kew, HO 45/14222.
63. Ibid., quoting from the Cabinet Papers, CP 143, Apr 1928.
64. *Daily Telegraph*, 18 July 1928.

country.'[65] He concluded, using comments that had circulated Whitehall for several years, that:

> The position as I see it, and as the Government see it, has been Materially changed since the development of greyhound racing since 1926. There are only seven horse racecourses within 15 miles of Charing Cross, with 187 days of racing, whereas in the same area there are 23 greyhound tracks with over 4,000 days racing within a year. Greyhound racing has brought on-the-course betting facilities, often as almost a nightly event, into most of the large urban centres of the country.[66]

There was, indeed, alarm at the prospects that greyhound racing offered to working-class gambling.

Both the NAGL and the Government worried about the impact of greyhound racing on women and children and the way in which it encouraged a 'something for nothing' attitude. In 1927 the Home Office received reports that of all attendees at greyhound meetings '30 per cent were women and girls'.[67] In 1934 various parliamentarians noted the facilities offered for children. The Cartyne track, near Glasgow, had established a nursery 'So that mothers can leave their children in the nursery while they go and gamble' and Harringay track, in North London, provided an equipped playground where children could be left: '[t]wo see-saws, and a round sandpit complete with spades and buckets are some of the amusements provided for kiddies.'[68] John McGovern, the Independent Labour Party MP for Glasgow Shettlestone in which the Cartyne track was

---

65. *Parliamentary Debates*, Commons, 1954, vol. 292, 27 June 1954, col. 1137.
66. Ibid.
67. The National Archives of the UK at Kew, HO 45/14222, 7 Oct 1927 file.
68. *Parliamentary Debates*, Commons, 1934, vol. 292, 27 June 1934, col. 1139, from the statements of T. Williams, Labour MP for Don Valley.

situated, agreed that it was 'a most degrading sight' to see women taking their children to the nurseries on this track.[69]

Nevertheless, the main criticism was that many greyhound tracks were running unregulated, and possibly illegal, totalisators where the owners determined how much of the total fund arising from all those who bet would be returned in winnings. As already noted many greyhound tracks ran their own totalisator in competition with the track bookies between 1928 and 1933, when they were found to be illegal, and from 1934 onwards when they operated under the conditions and controls of the 1934 Betting and Lotteries Act. Prior to 1933 the owners often kept about twelve per cent of the tote fund from bets for their expenses and profits but after the 1934 Act that was restricted to six per cent of the fund. Prior to 1934 there were claims of exploitation by the owners of the tracks who set up their own totalisators. Indeed, it was claimed of a Manchester company formed in 1931 (presumably the White City in Manchester although it could have been the Salford Albion) using a totalisator that it:

> ... in 1931 declared a dividend of £212,000. One man invested £100 and has been paid £6,000 a year ever since. Another guaranteed the company at the bank for a few thousand pounds, and he has drawn over £7,000 a year ever since. These fellows ought to be on the means test and know the meaning of poverty. King Solomon's mines cannot compare with the money that has been raked out of greyhound racing and yet these people tell us that it is clean, honest and fair as any sport.[70]

In effect, then, the decade between the mid-nineteen twenties and the mid-nineteen thirties saw government, the Home Office and Parliament fear the increasing opportunities for working-class gambling and doubt whether or not licensing gambling could be successful. It was these fears and concerns

---

69. Ibid., col. 1212.
70. Ibid., col. 1158.

that appear to have checked the liberalising attitude of the police and the Home Office. Yet, after another quarter of a century off-course ready money gambling was legalised through the licensing of betting offices.

Between the 1930s and 1960 the attitudes towards gambling changed. Most of this seems to have occurred after the Second World War for at this time gambling on the pools and greyhound racing was strictly controlled – the football pools being reduced to about a fifth of their late nineteen thirties level and gambling on greyhound racing being reduced slightly between 1930 and 1942 before recovering strongly.[71] In the late nineteen forties the situation of working-class gambling did not change much but in the nineteen fifties and the nineteen sixties there were widespread cultural and legal changes occurring in British society – connected with sexuality, censorship, abortion, music and other cultural features – that marked these years out as a period of liberalisation. In addition, the final report of the Royal Commission on Betting, Lotteries and Gambling (1949–51), better know as the Willink Report, contained a chapter on 'The Social Effects of Gambling' which concluded that gambling was generally not dangerous to the individual, family and community unless taken to excess: 'It is the concern of the State that gambling, like other indulgences such as drinking of alcoholic liquor, should be kept within reasonable bounds, but this does not imply that there is anything inherently wrong in it.'[72] It therefore concluded that the prohibition of off-course ready money gambling was 'difficult to enforce, it has become out of date as a result of the development of many other forms of legal gambling, it gives an appearance of class distinctions, and is clearly ineffective as a method of checking gambling ...' It added that most witnesses felt that there was a need for a change in the law and that 'the

71. Laybourn, *Working-Class Gambling in Britain*, chapter four and particularly pp. 164, 189.
72. The Royal Commission on Betting, Lotteries and Gaming (1949-51), *Report*, 159.

continued prohibition of cash betting off course is neither necessary nor desirable'.[73]

In addition, by the nineteen fifties most political parties were using the 1934 Betting and Lotteries Act to run their own bingo, card clubs and other lottery money-raising activities. The Labour Party did this on a grand scale between about 1947 and 1953, before it became clear that in many cases they were breaking the law by running illegal public lotteries rather than the legal private lotteries permitted by the 1934 Act. In fact a Labour Party lottery survey in 1954 suggests that about a third of the Labour Party constituency agents would lose their posts if the lottery (lotteries including bingo, whist, and some other card games) was stopped.[74] Gaming had become part of the accepted culture of political parties, and it is not surprising that the Conservative government and the opposition parties operated together to get the Small Lotteries and Gaming Act passed through Parliament in 1955 and 1956, in the hope that it would legalise their fund-raising activities.

On 25 November 1955 Ernest Davies, Labour MP for Enfield, promoted his private member's Small Gaming Bill to rectify the confusing situation about lotteries or games of chance. He stated that 'The laws of betting, lotteries and gaming are so complex, confusing and muddled in character and interconnected and so unequal in their incidence that the law is completely out of line with public opinion and common practice.[75] He added that a vicar could run a raffle at a church bazaar but that if he sold a ticket outside the church hall, or inside it before the local MP had opened the bazaar, 'he is in danger of being hauled off in a Black Maria.' Indeed, Davies

---

73. Ibid., 213.
74. Laybourn, *Working-Class Gambling in Britain*, pp. 261–306; Laybourn, '"There Ought not to be One Law"', 215–16; Labour Party Archives and Study Centre, Manchester, LPNAD (Labour Party National Agents Department), Betting and Lotteries file 1947–1970.
75. *Parliamentary Debates*, Commons, 1955, vol. 546, 25 Nov 1955, col. 1894.

argues that if he, the lord chancellor, the home secretary, and the Chief Justice, played a rubber of bridge for so much as 1s. per hundred they 'will be in danger of appearing before the beak at Marlborough next morning. The same state of affairs applies to lotteries run by clubs.'[76]

The Small Gaming Act of 1956 allowed clubs and political organisation to offer better prices and to allow the public to join in bingo and other lotteries in the private clubs. It also set down the conditions for offering monetary prices. Unfortunately, however, it led to confusion. The 1934 Betting and Lottery Act allowed private lotteries to raise money for private clubs. The 1956 Act allowed the public into lotteries operated by clubs but did not allow the profits to be used for the benefit of the members of the private clubs; they could only be used for charity. This difference led to many clubs operating illegally by using the 1956 proceeds for their own members. In the end it proved necessary to clarify this situation again and in the wide-ranging Betting and Gaming Act of 1960 the Conservative government also took the opportunity to replace the 1906 Street Betting Act by introducing the licensed off-course book betting office. The decision to do this had already been taken in Cabinet. Harold Macmillan, the Prime Minister, wanted a bill to regulate bookmakers by licensing them and allowing the formation of betting offices, a bill which would also 'bring the tangled law on gaming into line with what is thought to be contemporary public opinion'.[77] In effect it was implementing the findings of the Royal Commission on Betting, Lotteries and Gaming (1949–51) which had suggested the creation of licensed betting offices. Times had changed and the religious anti-gambling lobby, though still present, could not stop this move. In the end government had come to accept that it was not possible to impose a law that was flouted on a regular daily basis by a majority of the population in a democratic state.

---

76. Ibid., col. 1805.
77. The National Archives of the UK at Kew, PREM 1/2004, 1953–1960 file, Report of Sir Charles Cunningham on the discussion with the Prime Minister, 23 Oct 1959, p. 5.

The central argument of this chapter is that in the early twentieth century the working classes generally acted with restraint when it came to gambling and gaming, a view advocated by Carl Chinn and Mark Clapson who accept that the working classes liked 'a bit of a flutter'. It rejects the view of the NAGL that the working classes gambled to excess and that this resulted in deleterious social and economic consequences. Rather it maintains the ubiquity of gambling which was an integral part of working-class life.

The NAGL was successful in getting the blatantly discriminatory Street Betting Act passed in 1906 but it soon proved to be unenforceable. Indeed, by the nineteen twenties most chief constables and the Home Office wanted the removal of the Act. The opposition of the Labour Party, however, still partly present after 1931, and the rising concern about the mushroom growth of the football pools greyhound racing and the Irish Hospital Sweepstake Lottery undermined the attempts to remove the 1906 Act during the inter-war years. However, this could not last forever. By the 1950s British society was changing rapidly and the Royal Commission on Betting, Lotteries and Gaming (1949–51) had concluded that the 1906 Street Betting Act, and indeed the 1853 Betting Houses Act, were no longer relevant in a modern changing society.

It is here that I return to my own starting point. In the nineteen fifties I could not understand why off-course ready money gambling on horses was illegal. Equally I couldn't understand why policemen would raid illegal bookmakers one day and place a bet with them the next. I couldn't see why whist drives were illegal when they were so often used to raise money for local events, including the celebration of the Queen's coronation in 1953. Why was it wrong for the working class to enjoy the same rights as the middle classes?

My research has indicated no great plot or conspiracy against the working classes but that there are many twists and turns in government attitudes. The actions of the Home Office, the impact of anti-gambling forces, the attitudes of the police, the evidence gathered for royal commissions and select committees, all ensured that there is no straight course in the evolution of British social policy. These factors dictated the pace of events, and the oscillations in policy, but they did not necessarily dictate its direction; that was more conditioned by the needs of an increasingly democratising society which ultimately aimed to reduce social inequality.

The working classes saw gambling and gaming as part of their contribution to this process of reducing inequalities in life. It was regarded by many of them as a form of self-help which could liven up their lives and offer them the occasional financial windfall to alleviate temporarily their poor economic situation. As Rowntree reflected at the end of the inter-war years, the working classes were often 'in search of phantom fortunes' but they were also realistic enough to know that their flutters were likely to bring only limited rewards. Small flutters for small rewards became part of the fabric of the economy and leisure of working-class households in the first six decades of the twentieth century.

Bibliography

I Primary

(a) Unpublished

Birmingham, University of Birmingham: Heslop Room. Chinn Interviews with bookmakers, Mr. Jordan Tape 296 a and b; Mr Cooper 319 a and b; Jack Ingham 414 a and b.

London, The National Archives of the UK at Kew. HO 45/14222; HO 45/14616; HO 45/ H0 45/20540; HO 45/24919; HO/10301/117059, HO 320/12, HO 335/32; HO 320/34; CAB 23, CP 143, PREM 1/2004

Manchester, Newton St, Greater Manchester Police Museum. Betting Log Book, Salford area

Manchester, Labour History and Study Archive Centre. Labour Party National Agents Department (LPNAD), Betting and Lotteries file 1947–70.

York, Borthwick Institute, University of York. Rowntree, B. S., collection on gambling in the Joseph Rowntree Foundation Library.

(b) Published

Barnsley British Co-operative Society, *The Coronation History of the Barnsley British Co-operative Society Limited, 1892–1902* (Manchester: Co-operative Wholesale Society's Printing Works, 1903).

The Barnsley Chronicle.

Barnsley College of Technology, *Guide to Courses available at Barnsley College of Technology* (1962).

Barnsley College of Technology, *Barnsley College of Technology Prospectus* (1962–63).

Barnsley College of Technology, *Barnsley College of Technology Prospectus 1963–4.*

Barnsley Education Committee, *Annual Distribution of Prizes and Report on 11 December 1912 given by the Secretary and Head Master of the Technical School and Evening Continuation Schools.*

The Barnsley Independent.

Barnsley Official Guide 1937 (Barnsley, 1937, published as part of the Joy Week Magazine).

Barnsley Mining and Technical College, *Opening Ceremony of the New Mining and Technical College 1932.*

Barnsley Technical School Magazine, No.1, Vol. 1 (Jan 1912).

Barnsley School of Arts and Crafts, *Official Opening of Fairfield House 1946.*

The Bradford Observer.

Central Public Opinion Poll, 1945.

Daily Express Research, 1948.

His Majesty's Inspectors of Schools, *Inspection Report for 1936 Barnsley Mining College.*

MacDonald, J. R., *Ideal Citizenship* (London, 1905).

Manchester Guardian.

The Municipal Review (Sept 1931).

New Chronicle.

National Anti-Gambling League, *Bulletin.*

Ordnance Survey Map of Barnsley, 1:2500, one inch to one mile (1962).

Parliamentary Debates, House of Commons, various references from 1906 to 1955.

Perkins, E. Benson, *The Problem of Gambling* (London: Epworth Press, 1919).

—— *Betting Facts: Being an Account of the Facts on Betting Given in Evidence before the Select Committee of the House of Commons on Betting Duty* (London: Student Christian Movement, 1925).

—— *Gambling and Youth* (London: National Sunday School Union, 1933).

—— *Gambling in English Life* (revised edn, London: Epworth Press, 1950).

Ranger, William, 'The Privy Accommodation', *Ranger Report* (London: George E. Eyre and William Spottiswood, 1852).

Rowntree, B. Seebohm, *Poverty and Progress: A Second Social Survey of York* (London: Longmans, Green, 1941).

Royal Commission on Lotteries and Betting (1932–33), Cmnd 4234, *Interim Report*; also *Minutes.*

Royal Commission on Betting, Lotteries and Gaming (1949–51), *Final Report* (London: HMSO, 1951).

Select Committee of the House of Lords (1901–02), *Minutes.*

Select Committee on Betting Duty, 1923, *Report.*

Sketches of Early Barnsley (Barnsley, 1901).

The Society of Arts Journal, 1852–58.

The Times.

Yorkshire Union of Mechanics' Institutes, *Annual Reports.*

II Secondary

Alliott, Gerald J., *The Vanishing Relics of Barnsley* (Barnsley: Wharncliffe Publishing, 1996).

Argles, M., *South Kensington to Robbins: An Account of English Technical and Scientific Education since 1851* (London: Longmans, 1964).

Benson, John, 'Coalminers, coalowners and collaboration: the miners' permanent relief fund movement in England, 1860–1895', *Labour History Review*, 68 (2003), pp. 181–94.

Black, Alistair, and Hoare, Peter (eds), *The Cambridge History of Libraries in Britain and Ireland*, iii: *1850–2000* (Cambridge: Cambridge University Press, 2006).

Brodie, Antonia, et al. (eds), *Directory of British Architects, 1834–1914* (London: Continuum, 2001).

Brown, B., 'Typography and artificial memory', in M. Gorman, *Typography New Era New Language: An International Conference on the Teaching and Practice of Typography* (Manchester: Righton Press, 1995), pp. ??–??.

Chinn, C., *Better Betting with a Decent Feller: A Social History of Bookmaking* (London: Aurum, 2004)

Clapson, M., *A Bit of a Flutter: Popular Gambling and English Society, c. 1823–1961* (Manchester: Manchester University Press, 1992).

Cross, Claire M., 'A Yorkshire religious house and its hinterland: Monk Bretton Priory in the sixteenth century', in Simon Ditchfield (ed.), *Christianity and Community in the West: Essays for John Bossy* (Aldershot: Ashgate, 2001), pp. 72–86.

Davies, Andrew, *Leisure, Gender and Poverty: Working-Class Culture in Salford and Manchester, 1900–39* (Buckingham: Open University Press, 1992).

Elliott, Brian, *Barnsley's History from the Air* (Barnsley: Wharncliffe Publishing, 1994).

Elliott, Brian, *A Century of Barnsley* (Stroud: Sutton, 2000).

Elliott, Brian, 'Glimpses of Mediaeval Barnsley', in Brian Elliott (ed.), *Aspects of Barnsley*, 7 (Barnsley: Wharncliffe Books, 2002).

Farnsworth, Stephen, and Glister, Roger, *Barnsley Buses* (Barnsley: Wharncliffe Books, 2001).

Gliddon, Paul, 'Politics for Better or Worse: Political Nonconformity, the Gambling Dilemma and the North of England Newspaper Company, 1903–1914', *History*, 87 (2002), pp. 227–44.

Gosden, P. H. J. H., and Sharp, P. R., *The Development of an Education Service: The West Riding, 1889–1974* (Oxford: Martin Robertson, 1978).

Griffin, Colin, 'Not just a case of baths, canteens and rehabilitation centres: the Second World War and the recreational provision of the Miners' Welfare Commission in coalmining communities', in Nick Hayes and Jeff Hill (eds), *'Millions like us'? British Culture in the Second World War* (Liverpool: Liverpool University Press, 1999), pp. 261–94.

Hill, Alan, *The South Yorkshire Coalfield* (Stroud: Tempus, 2001).

Holland, Phil, and Smith, Mark, *Memories of Barnsley: Nostalgic Photographs of Local Places, People and Events, 1930 to 1970* (Halifax: True North Books, 1997).

Hudson, J. W., *The History of Adult Education* (1851; London: Woburn Press, 1969).

Jepson, N. A., *The Beginnings of English University Adult Education: Policy and Problems: A Critical Study of the Early Cambridge and Oxford University Extension Lecture Movements between 1873 and 1907, with Special Reference to Yorkshire* (London: Joseph, 1973).

Johnston, Rose, 'George Orwell and the Road to Pogmoor Sands', in Brian Elliott (ed.), *Aspects of Barnsley*, 5 (Barnsley: Wharncliffe Publishing, 1998).

Jones, Melvyn, 'The Migration History of a Linen Weaving Family, 1798–1932', in Brian Elliott (ed.), *Aspects of Barnsley*, 6 (Barnsley: Wharncliffe Books, 2000).

Kelly, Thomas, *A History of Education in Great Britain* (Liverpool: Liverpool University Press, 1962).

Lawson, J., *The Man in the Cap: The Life of Herbert Smith* (London: Methuen, 1941).

Laybourn, Keith, *Working-Class Gambling in Britain c. 1906-1960s: The Stages of Political Debate* (Lewiston N.Y.: Edwin Mellen Press, 2007).

Laybourn, Keith, '"There Ought not to be One Law for the Rich and Another for the Poor which is the Case To-day": The Labour Party, Lotteries, Gaming, Gambling and Bingo c. 1900–1960s', *History*, 93 (2008), pp. 201–23.

Lewis, Brian, Dyke, Mel, and Clayton, Ian, *The Bus to Barnsley Market: Journeys into Experience* (Castleford: Yorkshire Arts Circus, 1989).

Lewis, Brian, Sawyer, Ian, Stevenson, Lans, and Vernon, Colleen *Barnsley Seams of Gold* (Barnsley: Open College of the Arts, 2001).

Maclure, J. Stuart, *Educational Documents: England and Wales 1816 to the Present Day* (1965; 3rd edn, London: Methuen, 1973).

McCord, Norman, *British History 1815-1906* (Oxford: Oxford University Press, 1991).

Pevsner, Nikolaus, *The Buildings of England, Yorkshire West Riding* (Harmondsworth: Penguin, 1967).

Pollard, Richard, and Pevsner, Nikolaus, *Lancashire: Liverpool and the South West* (New Haven and London: Yale University Press, 2006).

Rosenthal, T. G., 'Paula Rego: Complete Graphic Works', in P. Coldwell, *Paula Rego Printmaker* (London: Marlborough Graphics. (London: Thames and Hudson, 2005)

Sillitoe, Helen, *A History of the Teaching of Domestic Subjects* (London: Methuen & Co., 1933).

Sutherland, Gillian, 'Education', in F. M. L. Thompson (ed.), *The Cambridge Social History of Britain, 1750-1950* (3 vols, Cambridge: Cambridge University Press, 1990).

Tasker, E. G., *Barnsley Streets* (4 vols, Barnsley: Wharncliffe Books, 2001).

Taylor, Kate, *Barnsley Cinemas* (Loughborough: Mercia Cinema Society, 2008).

Tylecote, M., *The Mechanics' Institutes of Lancashire and Yorkshire Before 1851* (Manchester: Manchester University Press, 1957).

Vernon, Anne, *A Quaker Business Man: The Life of Joseph Rowntree, 1836–1925* (London: George Allen & Unwin, 1958).

Walker, M. A., *Examinations for the 'Underprivileged' in Victorian Times: the Huddersfield Mechanics' Institution and the Society for the Encouragement of Arts, Manufactures and Commerce* (Northwood: The William Shipley Group for the Royal Society of Arts, 2008).

Wilkinson, Joseph, *History of Worsbrough* (London: Farrington & Co.; Barnsley: T. Lingard, 1872).

(b) Unpublished Secondary Sources

Luckhurst, K. W., 'Some Aspects of the History of the Society of Arts' (unpubl. Ph.D. thesis, University College London, 1957).

Walker, M. A., 'A Solid and Practical Education within the Reach of the Humblest Means: The Growth and Development of the Yorkshire Union of Mechanics' Institutes 1838–1891' (unpubl. Ph.D. thesis, University of Huddersfield, 2008).

(c) Website

Gosden, Peter, 'Wilson, Lucy (1834–1891)', *Oxford Dictionary of National Biography* (Oxford: Oxford University Press, 2004).

Lowe, Roy, 'Sadler, Sir Michael Ernest (1861–1943)', *Oxford Dictionary of National Biography*.

Brodie, Marc, 'Smith, Herbert (1862–1938)', *Oxford Dictionary of National Biography* (Oxford: Oxford University Press, 2004), *sub nomine*.